T0058471

# Anti-Matter:

## Michel Houellebecq and
## Depressive Realism

# Anti-Matter:

Michel Houellebecq and
Depressive Realism

Ben Jeffery

Winchester, UK
Washington, USA

First published by Zero Books, 2011
Zero Books is an imprint of John Hunt Publishing Ltd., Laurel House, Station Approach,
Alresford, Hants, SO24 9JH, UK
office1@o-books.net
www.o-books.com

For distributor details and how to order please visit the 'Ordering' section on our website.

ISBN: 978 1 84694 922 7

A CIP catalogue record for this book is available from the British Library.

Design: Lee Nash


Printed in the UK by CPI Antony Rowe
Printed in the USA by Offset Paperback Mfrs, Inc

We operate a distinctive and ethical publishing philosophy in all
areas of our business, from our global network of authors to
production and worldwide distribution.

# CONTENTS

Introduction: Depressive Realism                          1

1. Against the World, Against Life                         5
2. What Good are Books?                                   21
3. Your Imagination is a Liar                             37
4. Everything and Nothing                                 54
5. Utopia                                                 59
6. There is Actually No Such Thing as Atheism             76

Notes                                                     93

*For my parents*

# Introduction: Depressive Realism

The idea that life is fundamentally not good, and cannot be fixed, has a prestigious history in Western arts and letters. The *Iliad* and the tragedies of Aeschylus and Sophocles provide unflinching visions of human misery and common helplessness against fate. From the English canon, *King Lear* is perhaps the work of unromanticised pain *par excellence*. Pessimism is exemplified in the Christian tradition by the writings of Blaise Pascal and the outlook of the Puritans (people who 'hated life and scorned the platitude that it is worth living', in H.P. Lovecraft's admiring words). Arch-pessimist Arthur Schopenhauer devoted an entire philosophy to the aim of demonstrating that existence was necessarily bad, driven by an unceasing, unquenchable, thoughtless cosmic Will to which we are all puppets, and by which we are inevitably destroyed. 'Life is a business that does not cover its costs', he said – all is not for the best in the workings of the universe. We are thrown into the middle of a world we do not understand and cannot control. Our desires are mad and forever outstrip our means of satisfying them. Reality is something we must constantly repress in order to function.

What all varieties of pessimism have in common is the principle that the truth is undesirable – that unhappiness coincides with the loss of illusions, and that, conversely, happiness is a type of fantasy or ignorance. In *The Varieties of Religious Experience* (1902), on the subject of optimism, William James wrote: 'The method of averting one's attention from evil, and living simply in the light of the good is splendid as long as it will work. It will work with many persons; it will work far more generally than most of us are ready to suppose'. But, he adds:

there is no doubt that healthy-mindedness is inadequate as a philosophical doctrine, because the evil facts which it refuses positively to account for are a genuine portion of reality; and they may after all be the best keys to life's significance, and possibly the only openers of our eyes to the deepest levels of truth.

The normal process of life contains moments as bad as any which insane melancholy is filled with, moments in which radical evil gets its innings and takes its solid turn. The lunatic's visions of horror are all drawn from the material of daily fact. Our civilization is founded on the shambles, and every individual existence goes out in a lonely spasm of helpless agony. If you protest, my friend, wait until you arrive there yourself.

In his essay 'Mourning and Melancholia' (1917), Sigmund Freud entertained the thought that depressive melancholy was a kind of sickness-by-truth, something that happens whenever a person is unable to tell themselves the lies needed for getting up and going about their daily business. Freud accepted that depression was a pathological disorder, but just because someone is afflicted with an abnormal amount of self-loathing it does not follow that the feeling is unjustified:

It would be... fruitless from a scientific and a therapeutic point of view to contradict the patient who levels such reproaches against his ego in this way. In all likelihood he must in some way be right... He seems only to be grasping the truth more keenly than others who are not melancholic... [If] he describes himself as a petty, egotistic, insincere and dependent person, who has only ever striven to conceal the weakness of his nature... he may as far as we know come quite close to self-knowledge and we can only wonder why one must become ill in order to access to such truth.

The psychotherapist Gary Greenberg comments: 'Some melancholics may be mistaken... but the validity of their self-evaluations is not germane to the question of whether they are suffering from melancholy. The true mark of illness is the melancholic's failure to maintain the sense that he is not petty, egotistic, etc., *even if he is.*'

The idea that lucidity and mental well-being are not coincident has found some support in modern science. The term 'depressive realism' comes from a psychological study performed by Alloy and Abramson in 1979 which suggested that depressives routinely demonstrate better judgment about how much control they have over events (as opposed to non-depressives, who habitually over-estimate their control). Alloy and Abramson concluded that 'depressed people are "sadder but wiser"... Non-depressed people succumb to cognitive illusions that enable them to see both themselves and their environment with a rosy glow.'

What follows is not a systematic study of depression or a history of pessimistic thought. The idea of depressive realism is fascinating, however, and I'm interested in the various methods we have for dispelling or staving off pessimism – a task nearly all of us will need (or have needed) to perform at some time in our lives. William James's observation strikes me as undeniably true. It is generally easier not to think about all of the bad things that go on in the world. But bad things really do happen, and even very sheltered lives will experience periods of awful bitterness, frustration, loss and unhappiness. Then, at the end, you die – just like everybody else. Even if you are inclined toward the view that pessimism is self-indulgent, idle, decadent, or the preserve of weak-wills (and arguably it is all of these things), you would have to admit there are some good reasons for taking a dim view of existence.

The inspiration for this essay, and its principal focus, is the French author Michel Houellebecq. *Anti-Matter* could be described as a piece of extended literary criticism, and that would be sort of right, but it would be more exact to say it uses Houellebecq's novels as a basis for thinking about pessimism and how it relates to honesty, how novelists justify their work, what people think art is for, and philosophical materialism, amongst other things. I would like to thank Keith Jeffery and Lucy Campbell for their help reading and commenting on my manuscript, and Caoimhe McAlister for her invaluable translation work. Special thanks to Mark Fisher and to Jon Baskin and the rest of the *Point* magazine editorial staff, without whom this book would not have been written.

# Against the World, Against Life

Michel Houellebecq has published five novels, all of them bitter and miserable. Their pessimism isn't the only thing to them, or necessarily the most important thing, but it is probably the first that you'll notice. *Extension du domaine de la lutte* (1994), *Les Particules élémentaires* (1998), *Plateforme: Au Milieu du Monde* (2001), *La Possibilité d'une Île* (2005) and *La Carte et le Territoire* (2010) – published in Britain as *Whatever, Atomised, Platform* and *The Possibility of an Island* (at time of writing, *La Carte et le Territoire* has yet to appear in English) – are callow, cynical, sex-obsessed, openly racist and misogynistic in turn, rife with B-grade porn writing, contradictory, full of contempt for art and intellectuals, and operate on a kind of low masculine anger at the indignities of being beta-chimp. They are nonetheless serious, and owe their reputation to artistic achievement as much as any naughty thrill they elicit. Translated into over twenty-five languages, Houellebecq has won the Dublin IMPAC award (the world's most lucrative single-book prize) and the Prix Novembre for *Atomised*, the 1999 Grand Prix national de lettres, the Prix Interallié for *The Possibility of an Island*, the Prix Goncourt for *La Carte et le Territoire*, and has sustained critical and popular attention during a decade and a half in which the number of writers to emerge from Europe with any sense of importance is next to zero. This comparatively huge success is worth some attention. Houellebecq's books are not historical romances or ripping thrillers. They are nakedly philosophical novels, embodying one of the more significant efforts by any contemporary writer to understand and communicate the tensions of our times, a great many of which are plainly hostile to the production of engaged literature.

*Whatever* was initially an underground hit, scoring respectable sales in France despite receiving almost no publicity. *Atomised* made Houellebecq famous, selling hundreds of thousands of copies and being debated on the front page of *Le Monde*. Each of his subsequent novels has been a major event in the literary press. He has published a novella, *Lanzarote* (2000), an extended essay on the life and work of H.P. Lovecraft, *H.P. Lovecraft: Against the World, Against Life* (1991), a book of poetry *The Art of Struggle* (1996), and a collection of letters exchanged with Bernard Henri-Lévy, *Public Enemies* (2008), all of which are available in English, plus various other collections of essays and poetry, which are not. There is an album for sale of Houellebecq singing some of his poems over rock music, and he personally directed the feature film adaptation of *The Possibility of an Island* (2008). This would be an impressive rate of capitalisation for *any* sort of writing career. That Houellebecq has achieved as much on the basis of such misanthropic novels is remarkable. They are unconventional books, without much literary flourish, animated by characters either clad in primary-colours or left indistinct (there are scarcely any memorable minor parts in Houellebecq). Which isn't to say that the prose isn't stylish: I've seen it described as 'geometrical', and there is something elegantly hard about the novels' terse, almost aphoristic passages of social and psychological observation. Houellebecq has a talent for generalisation. He is also filthy and often very funny with it. Julian Barnes was broadly right when he said that *Atomised* is a difficult book to describe without making it seem ponderous. There is a streak of perverse, satirical glee in Houellebecq that tends to get lost in summary, a pleasure not unlike listening to a very sharp friend being cruel about someone you privately dislike.

At the beginning of his first book, the biography of H.P. Lovecraft, Houellebecq set out his premises: 'No matter what might be said, access to the artistic universe is more or less entirely the preserve of those who are a little *fed up* with life.' Or more than a little:

> Life is painful and disappointing. It is useless, therefore, to write new realistic novels. We generally know where we stand in relation to reality and don't care to know any more. Humanity, such as it is, inspires only an attenuated curiosity in us. All these prodigiously refined 'notations,' 'situations,' anecdotes... All they do, once a book has been set aside, is reinforce the slight revulsion that is already nourished by any one of our 'real life' days.

Certainly these opening notes – those scare quotes around the words 'real life' – do not promise a wonderfully appetising read. But in fact Houellebecq's debut is a delight. *H.P. Lovecraft: Against the World, Against Life* is witty, sympathetic, beautifully written, and accomplishes the nicest thing a piece of criticism can: it makes you want to read what you are reading about. Lovecraft, a recluse whose single happy relationship was wrecked by his inability to find a salary, who wrote horror stories powered on (so Houellebecq argues) virulent racial hatred, exemplified in his life and work one of the engines of Houellebecq's own fiction: the refusal, or the failure, to develop into an adult. Lovecraft was convinced that the truth is the enemy of human interest. 'All rationalism tends to minimalize the value and the importance of life, and to decrease the sum total of human happiness', he wrote, in a letter quoted by Houellebecq. 'In some cases the truth may cause suicidal or nearly suicidal depression.' This sentiment is echoed throughout Houellebecq's work. However, the claim that it is 'useless... to write new realistic novels' is something he quickly retreated from. Without exception, Houellebecq's novels are concerned with the revulsion and hardship of quote-unquote real life.

What good is a 'realism' like that? It is easy enough, you

might think, to adopt a manful tone of voice and say that what matters in art is not wellbeing but truth, even if the truth is brutal and distressing. But if a piece of art is not only truthful but depressing and no good for you in its truthfulness, doesn't that sound like an excellent reason to avoid it? I'm not sure how to answer that question. Houellebecq's characters are defined by isolation and unhappiness, and they take these to be definitive rather than accidental parts of human existence. Their social relations are those of failure, determined by what they cannot relate to in others – 'It is in failure and through failure, that the subject constitutes itself,' as one puts it, and another: 'It is in our relations with other people that we gain a sense of ourselves; it is that, pretty much, that makes relations with other people unbearable' – all of which falls perilously close to navel-gazing. Whether in first- or third-person the Houellebecq hero (always male) typically takes the form of a soft-bodied, aging cynic who yearns exclusively for sex with young women and then spirals off into brooding monologues about the impossibility of living when it eludes him. The quantity of invective is high, particularly in *The Possibility of an Island*, easily the nastiest of the four titles. Its hero, a rich and famous comedian named Daniel, embarks on one affair with a woman that ends after they both agree that it would be futile to pretend that he could go on wanting her deteriorating body, and then another with a 22-year old nymphomaniac with whom he falls deeply in love, whilst maintaining that 'Like all very pretty young girls she was basically only good for fucking, and it would have been stupid to employ her for anything else, to see her as anything other than a luxury animal, pampered and spoiled, protected from all cares as from any difficult or painful task so as to be better able to devote herself to her exclusively sexual service'. Eventually she dumps him before running off to an orgy. Elsewhere, Daniel notes that: 'The dream of all men is to meet little sluts who are innocent but ready for all forms of depravity – which is what, more or less, all teenage girls are,' that 'living alone together is hell between consenting adults,' that 'legitimate disgust... seizes any normal man at the sight of a baby,' that 'a child is a sort of vicious dwarf, innately cruel, who combines the worst features of the species, and from whom domestic pets keep a wise distance', and so on.

If it isn't impossible for women to enjoy reading Houellebecq, it's true that there's a lot of junk in the way. Not only are his female characters viewed, and valued, almost exclusively in terms of desirability, Houellebecq unfortunately combines his urge to philosophise with an inability to come up with anything more profound than the idea that women are the only people capable of true empathy and love (when they aren't heartless, calculating, self-deluded snakes). And while it is strictly fallacious (not to mention lazy) to equate what an author writes with what an author thinks, it has to be said that there's a considerable amount of evidence that Houellebecq's novels really are all-about-him. Not only are his leading characters usually the same sort of guy, they are all guys who bear striking resemblances to their author. Two of them are called Michel. The early novels detail much of Houellebecq's life, pre-fame. *Platform* is a love story written shortly after he was married for the second time, and, as he approached fifty, Houellebecq released *The Possibility of an Island*, a book starring an embittered celebrity ruminating on the horrors of physical decline. Andrew Hussey, a friend of Houellebecq, has written in the *Observer* that 'his novels, to anyone who knows anything about him, are barely refracted versions of his life', and in a review of Denis Demonpion's biography, *Houellebecq non autorisé: enquête sur un phénomène*, in the *London Review of Books*, the critic Theo Tait remarks that, even though anyone could guess that there's strongly autobiographic current in Houellebecq's fiction, 'it's a shock... to learn quite how much of Houellebecq's life has been thrust raw – though often distorted – into his novels'. This includes characters in *Whatever* that turn out to be real people whose names have not been changed, depictions of Houellebecq's own parents, his childhood, his wives, his dog, his time in a mental institution, and (quoting Tait again) a litany of 'highly specific attacks on jobs, places and people that have, in one way or another, pissed him off'. The climax of this auto-plagiarism arrives in *La Carte et le Territoire*, where the novelist 'Michel Houellebecq' turns up as one of the characters ('a solitary man with strong misanthropic tendencies' who resembles 'a sickly old tortoise').

It is perfectly plausible that Houellebecq is a very self-absorbed man with toxic opinions, scarcely something that makes him unique as a novelist.[1] But there are purely aesthetic reasons for criticism besides. Like a lot of authors with a heavy intellectual agenda, Houellebecq has really just one big thing to say, and his trouble is finding ways to re-imagine it. The basic theory of negativity is laid out in *Whatever*, expanded and given narrative flesh in *Atomised*, and subsequently reset in the later novels. The first book you read by Houellebecq is therefore likely to be the one that makes the biggest impression, and those that follow, unless you are particularly sympathetic to his ideas, are more liable to try the patience and display flaws. As a work of art, *Atomised* is the most successful because it has the greatest momentum, and so it powers over most of the reader's incredulity. *The Possibility of an Island* – a long and caustic monologue against a cardboard backdrop – is the worst chiefly because it attains nothing like the same velocity.

Yet the best reason to read Houellebecq is that his work produces the scandalously rare impression of being relevant, of connecting to how life is, rather than how it might be if there were more adventures. Pessimism is unfalsifiable, of course, which is what makes it so often insipid. If someone is genuinely determined to look on the gloomy side of life there is no turning them about – the 'honesty' of a depressive realist is sapping and tedious in that way. All of Houellebecq's narrators present themselves as hard-headed men willing to speak unpleasant truths (explicitly, in *The Possibility of an Island*, where Daniel comments: 'On the intellectual level I was in reality slightly above average... I was just very honest, and therein lay my distinction; I was, in relation to the current norms of mankind, almost unbelievably honest'), but their stories would be banal if their author wasn't deft enough to make them plausible – that is, realistic. And it is hard, finally, to evade the conclusion that one big reason for Houellebecq's success is that enough people really do identify with these books; that they put into words things that people think and want to hear, but are either unable to articulate or unwilling to admit to. It's not a pleasant thought.

\*\*\*

In *Atomised* – the story of Bruno and Michel, two socially isolated half-brothers – tremendous pleasure is taken skewering neo-hippies and New Age mystics of all kinds. A thwarted hedonist, the 40-year-old Bruno spends a dismal fortnight holidaying in the Lieu du Changement, a semi-commune founded in 1975 with the aim 'of providing a place where like-minded people could spend the summer months living according to the principles they espoused.' It was 'intended that this haven of humanist and democratic feeling would create synergies, facilitate the meeting of minds and, in particular, as one of the founding members put it, provide an opportunity to "get your rocks off".' By the time Bruno visits in the late Nineties the Lieu du Changement has become miserable, a microcosm for one of Houellebecq's central themes – the cruelty and exclusion of the Sixties' sexual revolution. For the clientele of the Lieu, as 'they began to age, the cult of the body, which they had done so much to promote, simply filled them with disgust for their own bodies – a disgust they could see mirrored in the gaze of others... Dedicated exclusively to sexual liberation and desire, the Lieu naturally became a place of desperation and bitterness.' By the mid-Eighties the commune had become a corporate business, supplementing its promise of sexual liberty with quasi-religious workshops and esoteric disciplines. 'Tantric Zen, which combined vanity, mysticism and frottage, flourished.'

Bad luck in sex, the marginalisation of anyone who fails to be erotically desirable, is the backbone of Houellebecq's oeuvre. *Whatever*, the most overtly philosophical novel, is narrated by an unnamed computer technician (a job that Houellebecq held before he made his living as a writer) on a business trip training provincial civil servants how to use their new equipment. His companion is another young technician, Raphaël Tisserand. 'The problem with Raphaël Tisserand – the foundation of his personality, indeed – is that he is extremely ugly. So ugly that his appearance repels women, and he never gets to sleep with them.' The two men travel from town to town, retiring to bars and night-clubs after work, where Raphaël, affluent, but a total flop as a sexual commodity, meets progressively terrible frustrations. The issue, as the narrator diagnoses, is one of simple sexual economics: his colleague cannot offer anything on the market-place. 'Just like unrestrained economic liberalism, and for similar reasons, sexual liberalism produces phenomena of *absolute pauperisation*. Some men make love every day; others five or six times in their life, or never. Some make love with dozens of women, others with none. It's what's known as "the law of the market". … In a totally liberal sexual system certain people have a varied and exciting erotic life; others are reduced to mastur-bation and solitude.' Lacking charm and resembling a toad wrapped in cellophane, Raphaël has nothing he can trade. Characters that suffer because of their biological make-up, the life-sentence imposed by being undesirable, or the delayed punishment of aging, recur. Sex, we are told, is life's only real motive. If you are disqualified, or 'past it', then you will suffer unto death: 'All energy is of a sexual nature, not mainly, but exclusively, and when the animal is no longer good for reproducing, it is absolutely no longer good for anything.'

It is fair to say that Houellebecq doesn't shy away from what the author David Foster Wallace called 'the bizarre, adolescent belief that getting to have sex with whomever one wants whenever one wants is a cure for human despair'.[2] In fact Houellebecq can seem astonishingly naïve on the subject of sex, as though the pornographic is the only sort of fantasy he is unable to expose. In *The Possibility of an Island*, as in *Platform*, as in *Atomised*, whenever the hitherto alienated and frustrated hero finally finds his satisfaction – however fragile it may leave him, emotionally – the act is always phenomenal. No dispiriting failures to perform; no STDs or pregnancies; lots of excitingly acrobatic varieties and combinations; head-melting orgasms – everything exactly as advertised. 'Adolescent' is the word (really: a mixture of cynicism, erotic fantasising, vulgarity, and self-pity – how much more like a teenage boy could it get?). In mitigation, it's not as though Houellebecq isn't aware of this. His novels feed off a malaise about what it means to be adult, if anything beyond procreation. The vanguard of the Sixties and the sexual revolution were children refusing to grow up, idolising youth and freedom against traditional conceptions of responsibility. *Atomised* may shoot plenty of venom at their mythology, but Houellebecq's generation and all subsequent generations have inherited the idea that there is something vaguely bogus about maturity. 'I don't subscribe to the theory we only become *truly adult* when our parents die;' begins *Platform*, 'we never become truly adult.' Throughout, Houellebecq's fiction denigrates or omits one of the most basic forms of adult responsibility there is: parenthood. The narrator of *Platform*, viewing his father's coffin, tells us 'unpleasant thoughts came to me. He had made the most of his life, the old bastard; he was a clever cunt. "You had kids, you fucker..." I said spiritedly, "you shoved your fat cock in my mother's cunt." Well, I was a bit tense, I have to admit.' *Atomised* is a catalogue of bad parents and rotten children, one of the heroines dies trying to conceive, and – as in *The Possibility of an Island* – a hero candidly admits the neglect of his son:

> I work for someone else, I rent my apartment from someone else, there's nothing for my son to inherit. I have no craft to teach him, I haven't a clue what he might do when he's older. By the time he grows up, the rules I lived by will be meaningless – the world will be completely different. If a man accepts the fact that everything must change, then his life is reduced to the sum of his own experience – past and future generations mean nothing to him. That's how we live now. For a man to bring a child into the world now is meaningless. Women are different, because they never get past the need to have someone to love – which is certainly not true of men. … Kids are a trap, they are the enemy – you have to pay for them all your life – and they outlive you.

***

Raphaël Tisserand is killed in a car-accident, driving home in the mists on Christmas Eve. At his funeral: 'A few words were pronounced on the sadness of such a death and of the difficulty of driving in fog, people went back to work, and that was that.' But for the narrator of *Whatever*, who until then had taken a cold (if not gruesomely manipulative) attitude toward his partner, the news of Tisserand's death sparks a mental breakdown. After checking himself into a psychiatric hospital, the hero is confronted by a female counsellor who chastises him for speaking in overly abstract, sociological terms. His effort at self-analysis emerges: 'But I don't understand, basically, how people manage to go on living. I get the impression everybody must be unhappy; we live in such a simple world you understand. There's a system based on domination, money and fear [and there's a] system based on seduction and sex. And that's it. Is it really possible to live and believe that there's nothing else?' Afterwards, he asks the counsellor if she would sleep with him. She refuses.

It is not that Houellebecq is a reactionary writer exactly. For example, it is never suggested that religious faith is the solution to his character's dilemmas; the books are all resolutely atheist. The only places in which traditional religion makes a significant appearance are a subplot of *Whatever* – a Catholic priest, an old acquaintance of the narrator's, loses his faith over a failed affair with a young nurse – and at the climax of *Platform* in the form of Islamic terrorists.[3] In any case, as noted, Houellebecq's heroes are generally no less deviant than the sad revellers of the Lieu de Changement. What the sexual revolution stands for, rather, is the triumph of philosophical materialism: the world-view that erases the supernatural, making it impossible to believe in God and, at its logical conclusion, eradicating the possibility of communion altogether. The starkest material truth, after all, seems to be that we are all ultimately alone inside our skin, 'elementary particles'. In Houellebecq's fiction, the real brutality of post-Sixties sexual economics is that it is based on fact: that it is, in its way, progressive. One way of putting it is that in our enlightenment we are able to see ourselves as merely creatures, rather than God's creatures, and nature as purposeless matter, rather than divine plan. Humans are just animals, and, unsurprisingly, that knowledge gives precedence to biological impulse; to strength, health and beauty over weakness, infirmity and repulsiveness – and it makes self-interest paramount. Houellebecq's men find themselves incapable of considering anything but themselves, but they also apprehend, with some horror, the essential unsustainability of individualism. Living with nothing other than your own desires and urges makes their frustrations (increasingly awful and unavoidable as you age) tortuous – and the prospect of death is unmanageable. 'Contemporary consciousness is no longer equipped to deal with our mortality. More than at any time or in any civilisation, human beings are obsessed with aging. Each individual has a simple view of the future: a time will come when the sum of pleasures that life has left to offer is outweighed by the sum of pain (one can actually feel the meter ticking, and it ticks inevitably towards the end). This weighing up of pleasure and pain which, sooner or later, everyone is forced to make, leads logically, at a certain age, to suicide.' It is, to paraphrase Houellebecq on a different topic, an insoluble condition, but not really a complicated one.

'Old age; there was not a new blossoming at the end of the road, but a bundle of frustrations and sufferings, at first insignificant, then very quickly unbearable...' Even *The Possibility of an Island*, as bad as it is, achieves a kind of demonic power thanks to the intensity of its will to communicate the slide of bodily decay, 'the sadness of physical decrepitude, of the gradual *loss* of all that gave life meaning and joy':

> Not only did the old not have the right to fuck... rebellion was forbidden to them, rebellion too – like sexuality, like pleasure, like love – seemed reserved for the young and to have no point for other people, any cause incapable of mobilising the interest of young people was disqualified in advance, basically old people were in all matters treated simply as waste, to be granted only a survival that was miserable, conditional and more and more narrowly limited.

Esther, the narrator's 22-year-old mistress, never strikes the reader as much like an actual person, but the hero's desperation as their romance comes to an end – an end that he does not think he will survive – is palpable to the point of suffocation. You want to put the book down for air. It might be the paradigmatic scene in Houellebecq's fiction: the unbelievably desirable, sexually complicit Esther, source of incredible erotic ecstasies (and what's more: 'never with us had there been a question of using a condom, the subject had simply not been touched on'), described as compassionate and gentle by the narrator even though, bizarrely, he says that she could also not be expected 'to do any kind of favour for anyone' – an object of crippling love who does not love Daniel back, and finally abandons him without regret. Truly a fantasy woman, the fantasy inflated to absurd proportions for the sake of brute dramatic effect. Daniel is too old and soft for Esther and her friends, and they are too strong and free for him. 'I was wandering among them like some kind of prehistoric monster with my romantic silliness, my attachments, my chains.' Love is not a lie in Houellebecq's fiction, it is 'immense and admirable', the nearest thing there is to true communion, but in the end it is just another part of a battle you cannot help but lose. Houellebecq is hardly above mining sentiment on this score. Both *Platform* and *Atomised* strike a vein of classic romantic tragedy. Bruno's vacation in the Lieu is saved when he meets Christiane, a 40-year-old whose eyes 'were blue and a little sad', who travels to the Lieu for the sex rather than the mysticism. 'The whole spiritual thing makes the pick-up lines seem less brutal', she admits, but is unreservedly cynical about its value otherwise:

> I know what the veterans of 'sixty-eight are like when they hit forty, I'm practically one myself. They have cobwebs in their cunts and they grow old alone. Talk to them for five minutes and you'll see that they don't believe in any of this bullshit about chakras and crystal healing and light vibrations. They force themselves to believe it and sometimes they do for an hour or two... but then the workshop's over and they're still ugly, still ageing, still alone. So they cry for a bit – have you noticed? They do a lot of crying here.

In spite of his maladjustment and her damage, Bruno and Christiane find tenderness with one another. As their relationship progresses, Bruno's bleak worldview ('second-rate Neitzscheanism', he calls it) begins to thaw. The two fall in love. During a happy week together in Paris: 'They took a taxi to Les Halles and ate in an all-night brasserie. Bruno had rollmop herrings as a starter. "Now," he thought, "anything is possible." He had hardly done so when he realised that he was wrong.' What he thinks of is not a rival lover or external interference, but the course of nature, the implacable reality of separation and decline. The end that Bruno and Chistiane's affair eventually comes to, wrenching as it is, is only an accelerated version of the fate of all affairs: sooner or later the body fails. 'Though the possibilities were endless in his imagination... in reality his body was in a slow process of decay; Christiane's body was too. Despite the nights when they were as one, each remained trapped in individual consciousness and separate flesh. Rollmop herrings were clearly not the solution, but then again, had he chosen sea bass with fennel it would have been no different.' The burden of materialism, and by extension atheism, is that it is less – not more – able to manage suffering and evil than religiousness. Nature is indifferent to human interest, cold and amoral without a God to make it good. What remains once the divine or supernatural is eliminated is not a life devoid of meaning but a life whose meaning is essentially dependent on bodily function: health, pleasure and physical ability. By nature, those things expire, and the hardships of being a vulnerable, fearful, mortal human thing are left bare. It's no accident that once the Lieu de Changement's business began to sag (as its customers' bodies sagged) the Zen workshops arrived.

Houellebecq's individualism is after Bataille's maxim: an idea taken to its most terrible point. Thus the rejection of the family, which seems like one of the clearest fault-lines in Houellebecq's honesty (because how many parents never find honest joys in parenthood?), is consistent at least insofar as it makes self-interest – that 'iron-law' – the clear and dominant thing. The island alluded to in the title of *The Possibility of an Island* is love, conceived as a haven and a release from one's individuality. But it is always just an illusion of release, never a *real* possibility. Nonetheless, one is compelled by it. The revelation for Daniel is not that people are selfish, predatory animals (he affects to know this already) but how useless his cynicism has been. He loves Esther helplessly; he 'fell for it' all the same, and suffered the consequences. At its conclusion, *Possibility* traces the idea of love as a merging of two souls back to Plato. Wandering through a post-apocalyptic Spain, a remote descendant of Daniel's finds a fragment from the dialogue *Symposium* where Aristophanes is explaining his theory of love as a miraculous meeting between two mortal halves:

> I remembered perfectly what happens next [remarks Daniel's descendent after reading the fragment]: Hephaestos the blacksmith appeared to the two mortals 'while they were sleeping together', proposing to melt them and weld them together, 'so that from two they become only one, and that after their death, down there, in Hades, they will no longer be two, but one, having died a common death'. I remembered especially the final sentences: 'And the reason for this is that our former nature was such that we formed a complete whole. It is the desire and pursuit of this whole that we call love.'

With this reference, Houellebecq implies more than just antipathy to the *Symposium*'s vision of love. The Platonic dialogues are intertwined with the figure of Socrates, Plato's real-life teacher and principal dramatic character. In Socratic philosophy the physical world is only an imperfect copy of what is most real, which is an eternal, supreme heaven of forms and ideas. Knowledge of this heaven makes the soul just, and the man with a just soul cannot be harmed, said Socrates, because he can perceive that material suffering is unreal. It may be the most positive thought of all: the truth will make us safe. The crux of Houellebecqian dejection is that the truth does no such thing. There is nothing above us. It is humanism with a monstrous face.

The exception to Houellebecq's standard-template for protagonists is Michel Djerzinski, Bruno's half-brother. A scientist of genius, Michel has little in the way of normal human appetites. His work shows, 'on the basis of irrefutable thermodynamic arguments, that the chromosomal separation at the moment of meosis can create haploid gametes, in themselves a source of structural instability. In other words, all species dependent on sexual reproduction are by definition mortal.' The solution to this essential fallibility is to remake human material – the epilogue of *Atomised* tracks an epoch-shifting transformation as Djerzinski's genetic research lights the way to the creation of a race of sexless, benevolent, 'neo-human' immortals. The book ends with a tribute to humanity: a species that finally learned enough to be able and willing to engineer its own extinction.

# 2

# What Good are Books?

I was certain *Whatever* would provoke social change. Now I think it was megalomania... A novel won't ever change the world.

*Michel Houellebecq*


Part of the mythology of literature is that a great novel exists as a weather-vane to the age, informed by and informing the mood of the times, simultaneously symptomatic and diagnostic, reflecting the particular concerns of its spot in history, which, in turn, inform the deeper concerns of human life. The 'conceptual' difficulty for modern fiction, so to speak, might as well be termed the difficulty of realism. Since at least 1919, when Virginia Woolf published 'Modern Fiction', there has been a loose but persistent consensus among 'serious' writers that the world has changed in ways that makes Jane Austen-type classic realism inappropriate, so that if you really wanted to be realistic you would paradoxically find best expression in science-fiction or a postmodernist aesthetic, denying the possibility of realism as an achievable or desirable aim (cf. the critic Jerome Klinkowitz: 'If the world is absurd, and what passes for reality distressingly unreal, why spend time representing it?') The reasons for this steady, though now itself almost retro, shift in feeling are much-discussed but stubborn. Indeed one of the most striking things there is to notice reading popular criticism from the last half-century is how ghoulishly unaltered certain issues remain. Consider these three quotations:

'the principle of redundancy... is the principal affliction of modern life. ... Think of the sheer multiplication of works of art available to every one of us, superadded to the conflicting tastes and odors and sights of the urban environment that bombard our senses. Ours is a culture based on excess, on overproduction; the result is a steady loss of sharpness in our sensory experience. All the conditions of modern life – its material plenitude, its sheer crowdedness – conjoin to dull our sensory faculties.'

'for a writer of fiction to feel that he does not really live in his own country – as represented by *Life* or by what he sees when he steps out the front door – must seem a serious occupational hazard.'

'The task of the modern artist, as of the modern man, is to find something he can be sincere and serious in; something he can mean. And he may not at all.'

The first is from Susan Sontag's 'Against Interpretation', the second from Philip Roth's 'Writing American Fiction', and the third from Stanley Cavell's 'Music Discomposed' – essays published in 1964, 1961, and 1967, respectively. They are three good examples of worries that, in their essence if not their particulars (in the second quote, you could replace '*Life* magazine' with 'Google' and delete the need to leave the home), are as relevant today as when they were when they were written. Each of them speaks to a feeling of disorientation – of not knowing where to look, or what's important; a lack of clarity; lostness. The challenge for the modern writer is still, most urgently, one of finding her bearings. A similar point, if inflected, could be applied to many of the arts.

It is perfectly fair – and what's more, manifestly accurate – to say that Western social and cultural conditions are antithetical in lots of ways to creating literature that makes an impression on people in whatever way we mean when we say that it is 'engaged' or 'resonant'. A familiar way of putting it is to evoke a nefarious alliance of massively multiplied information sources and stimuli with a clustered and distracting mass-culture, and the corresponding shrinkage of the average person's attention-span and their willingness to isolate themselves with a book. The writer is caught in a double-bind: in order to properly capture the feel of a kinetic, overloaded world she must pack more, and more varied, material into her work, but does so for an audience that has less and less inclination to engage with it. Alternatively, the author simplifies and straightens her work in order to win readers, but at the expense of representing the world as she truly perceives it to be (i.e. selling-out). There is a concern that literature is simply unable to harmonise with an era where the written word has been so heavily marginalised by sound and image. Maybe the form is exhausted. Since there are only so many different ways to stick words together into a coherent whole, only so many styles to adopt, tones to take etc., might the last x-hundred years of cultural activity not have burnt up our artistic resources? These worries are all valid enough, and compounded by the fact that there has *never* been a moment where the novel was a pure and uncomplicatedly meaningful thing. Doubt about the efficacy of literature must be as old as the art itself. Redundancy, meaning joblessness or irrelevance, is a writer's special problem. Speaking generally, what literature aims to do is to convey or impose meaning, and this is what redundancy undermines, precisely why irrelevance is one of writing's natural terrors. Because literature is rooted in illusion and make-believe (basic fraudulence, in other words) and because asking what art is *for* is akin to asking what life is for (which is to say: have your pick of answer, good luck finding any proof), it is also a terror that is insoluble. For a neat expression of the awful sense of uselessness that anyone with a commitment to the written word must feel from time to time, Philip Larkin's immortal phrase would be hard to better: 'Books are a load of crap'. To devote even a part of your life to words is, inevitably, to wonder why you bothered.

However, the death of the novel has been declared so many times it would be meaningless to keep insisting on it. In any case, whatever 'the death of the novel' was supposed to stand for, it clearly wasn't the end of books, which continue to be published and consumed in large numbers. Perhaps it would be more useful to speak of the deadening of the novel, or of its un-death – à la some horror movie zombie – in which the industry rolls on, literature is still written and read, but some vital essence has been sucked away. At one stage, through sheer lack of competition, the novel was a premier source of social data: Dostoyevsky could be used to discover what life was like in prison, Dickens for life inside a workhouse, E.M. Forster for a picture of India, and so on. Now, television, radio, the internet, films, academia, research groups, major newspapers etc. all do a far superior job of collecting and spreading information, and so it would be stupid for people to choose fiction as a medium for news. Nor are prosperity and social comfort straightforward blessings for writers. In a 1996 *Harper's* essay about social novels, 'Perchance to Dream' (republished as 'Why Bother?' in his collection *How to be Alone*), Jonathan Franzen speculated that since so few terrible things have happened to America as a country, art has always had a tenuous purchase on the American imagination. 'The one genuine tragedy to befall us was slavery,' he remarked, 'and it's probably no accident that the tradition of Southern literature has been strikingly rich and productive of geniuses. (Compare the literature of the sunny, fertile, peaceful West Coast.)' As any beginner's creative writing class will tell you, conflict is what makes narrative go. Accordingly, cultural wounds are priceless bits of material for any novelist trying to tap into her society's secret desires and fears. But, superficially at least, the recent history of the West matches right up to Franzen's guess about America: the last twenty years have been characterised by a near-total absence of immediate trauma, dominated by events that are difficult to 'see' from street-level, such as climate change, or the spread of cyberspace, or the War on Terror (fought – with a few exceptions – entirely beyond Western borders), or even the banking crisis, a recession that might have been conjured out of air for all that the untrained eye was able to discern. There are other trends whose problematic character is partly constituted by vagueness about whether they are internal or external issues, and the extent to which they belong to us – e.g. immigration and globalisation. It makes sense that ex-colonial and multiethnic work, drawing on the antagonisms of migration and cultural melding, should be such a rich seam of English-language literature since the Sixties. It has blood and sweat to work with.

In a different respect, the felt reality of the West is overwhelmingly huge. If you were forced on pain of injury to try and say *what* is characteristic of the present moment, one serviceable answer would be: we know more. Our collective awareness is tremendous. It increases. 'The pain of consciousness, the pain of knowing, grows apace', in Franzen's words. The sum total of human knowledge has long outstripped the capacities of any individual, however brilliant they might be (it being said that the last person to know everything there was to know was Leibniz, which isn't true, but would be bad enough even if it were – he died in 1716). As a thought experiment, consider any subject (e.g. cooking) that you could claim some knowledge of. Now consider how many people in the world could claim greater knowledge of that subject, how much expertise you lack. Broaden your thought to cover all the fields of science, sport, art, language, mathematics, commerce, engineering, philosophy, history, law, geography, medicine, technology, etc. Try to imagine how much you don't know, that is known. It is dizzying.

The expanse of human activity and enterprise, and our consciousness of that expanse, are vital ingredients for the modern novelist's stew. The problem being that this enormous weight of collected data – or, more accurately, the fact that we are ever-more aware that this gigantic weight of data is sitting out there, collected – has awkward consequences for writing novels. The first, most obvious one is this: there is so much stuff! Far too much to fit into any book, too much for any single talent: how could any lone novelist capture what the world feels like when she has such flimsy snares at her disposal? But the days when there was any clear distinction between the local and the exotic seem gone, and so the pressure mounts on the novelist to pack her work full of data and colour, to take her books globetrotting, evoke the sensation that there is more going on in the world faster and everywhere; the interconnected, networked, speeding, modern kaleidoscope. However, the actual breadth of the world – the diversity of character and locale that you could encounter just by spending an evening channel-hopping or browsing the internet – humbles the imagination, and it seems impossible to do it justice. The present isn't so much a moving target as a multitude of twisting slipping bodies that refuse to remain targets long enough to take aim.

A massive proportion of Western art in the late twentieth and early twenty-first century is a reaction to the feeling of overload. But for literature the issue isn't simply one of scale, as though in principle, and with enough imagination and effort, one could amass a large enough quantity of information plus character and put it all inside one long book. It is also a matter of fit. In some plain respects novels just seem like the wrong way to depict life in the information age. A linear narrative without explicit audio/visual accompaniment doesn't rest easily in the job of conveying a time and place animated by flickering bangs and whizzes. It not just the problem already sketched, i.e. the need to compete with all sorts of other, extremely colourful, forms of entertainment for an audience with less attention to give or the desire to give it. It is that literature aiming to be 'realistic' would have to depict all the up-to-the-minute parts of the twenty-first century which make it difficult for novels to be that. As though the timely, twenty-first century novel would have to somehow internalise those elements that make novels seem irrelevant and out of step – that is, represent (in a novel) a form of life that novels do not seem to be representative of; like pushing square pegs against round holes. What would a long story be like where the hero worked all day and then spent all his spare time on the internet? Possibly very interesting, but also hard to imagine; as a rule of thumb, novels struggle to capture information-age paraphernalia, and very often seem wooden when they try.[4] The problem of fit is more serious by far than the problem of scale, it's the difference between having a long and arduous job on your hands and having a job you are wrong for. Any novelist who feels their medium to be out of tune with the world around them is obvious prey for the fear of irrelevance. It's a big deal. It's what Roth meant by describing the feeling of un-belonging as a serious occupational hazard for the author. And of course it doesn't take a genius to join the dots and conclude that the really characteristic detail of information-age culture *is* the aforementioned failure of retention; the transience and slipperiness of data – the attention-deficit. Except that taking this as the subject of your fiction is to risk falling down the worst, most barren sort of rabbit-hole, wherein either the novelist tries to feed the good word to an audience numbed to stimuli, or she's preaching irony to the choir; satirising forgetfulness and insubstantiality in ways that will end up being as entirely flimsy and disposable as their targets. Here again is the dilemma: we live with realities that are maddeningly difficult to write about, but fiction that doesn't engage with them isn't literature that's about what it's like, especially, to live at the moment.

David Shields is surely correct when he says, in *Reality*

*Hunger* (2010), that no artist ever aims to be unrealistic, even when they deny realism. 'Every artistic movement from the beginning of time is an attempt to figure out a way to smuggle more of what an artist thinks is reality into the work of art.' The most abrasive and fantastic art is still designed to show something true. (Lovecraft's monsters do this, working as mirrors to human insignificance.) But artists are equally aware, perhaps writers most of all, that what they do is irreparably false. There's a shudderingly powerful fact of existence beyond, and before, all words. The feebleness of writing in comparison to this fact is so obvious. The novelist hopes that she's wrong (although she knows she isn't). She tries, with a pessimism born of desperate need, to believe that there is some unique value in writing, which can be cultivated and transferred back to actual lived-life (although she can never prove this). The cycles of self-doubt spin around. It should be easy to see how living in the information age makes it so much worse. The terrors of redundancy are part and parcel of the enterprise of fiction writing. What modern life does is amplify them. It has never been easier to feel anonymous, as an artist or a person. Michel Houellebecq's books, which don't take a massive amount of interest in the world buzzing around them, manage to convey this atmosphere extremely well: the gap between real life and life-as-advertised, and how the sense of disappointment it generates has perversely become a bit of a cultural norm. 'There are some authors who employ their talent in the delicate description of varying states of soul, character traits, etc' expounds the narrator of *Whatever*:

> All that accumulation of realistic detail, with clearly differen-
> tiated characters hogging the limelight, has always seemed
> like pure bullshit to me... The world is becoming more
> uniform before our eyes; telecommunications are improving;
> apartment interiors are enriched with new gadgets. Human
> relationships become progressively impossible, which greatly

reduces the quantity of anecdote that goes to make up a life. And little by little death's countenance appears in all its glory.

\*\*\*

In a 1958 interview with *The Paris Review*, Ernest Hemmingway said that there is a part of writing it does no good to talk about. This is a perfectly sensible thought. It's impossible to entirely convey what a piece of art means to you, just as it's impossible to convey consciousness whole. But our inarticulacy is also the fundamental reason why deep attachment to art can seem so stupid, why it gets so frustrating to try to explain what the 'real' worth of art is (even to oneself). What is there in literature beyond entertainment? If the answer is that literature is 'ennobling', 'a higher pleasure', 'food for the soul', 'a spiritual good', then the problem isn't hard to appreciate. Even if you took these phrases seriously, they don't really explain things so much as mark a limit of the ability to explain. You have to trust people to know what you mean.

The difficulty handling the concept of a soul (for an atheist or an agnostic) is illustrative of the general problem. 'Soul' is extremely attractive shorthand for all sorts of things: essential personhood; aspects receptive to and capable of artistic beauty, deep feeling, moral claims, integrity; the idea there is something inherently precious about each human life; and so forth – there is no secular term that works as a clean substitute. Perhaps 'humanity' is the nearest to equivalence, although at the very least it seems flatly unsuited for conveying the power and nuance of certain figures of speech (e.g. 'a lost soul', 'soulful', 'touching the soul'). Nonetheless, there is obviously, unavoidably, a sense in which 'soul' is compromised by its etymology, i.e. its religiousness. The suspicion must be that it is an embellishment, that though soul and its variations make nice turns of phrase they are not strictly accurate ways of speaking –

merely allusive, symbolic. But of course there is tension in thinking of the soul as 'merely' allusive or symbolic, as though one doesn't really mean it, when it is used to describe states that people generally find *extremely* meaningful. In a theology lecture I once attended the speaker (a priest) began by taking a poll of the students: 'How many of you would describe yourself as religious?' About a third of the students put their hands up. Then: 'How many of you would describe yourself as spiritual?' Three-quarters of the audience raised their hands. The lecturer thought this demonstrated the enduring relevance of religious thought. Be that as it may, perhaps all it indicated was that many people instinctively reach for religious (or religiously-tinged) ways of speaking about themselves even when they consciously reject religion, a muddled desire that emerges in relatively noncommittal terms like 'spiritual'. I doubt that many of the students who raised their hands the second time could have given much of an explanation of what they meant by it; not because they were stupid or inconsiderate, but because the concept of spirituality is essentially murky, and it is hard to say what is serious about it if it is not a sort of comfort-blanket. 'Soul' is a particularly vivid example just because it shows its supernatural colour whilst being deeply embedded in our habits of speech. It seems to signify, or at least gesture toward, something very important – one feels as though it *must* mean something – and also to appear weirdly insubstantial, as though there is nothing behind it to make it real. A religious mindset might accommodate a more opaque notion of explanation, giving the impenetrability of certain concepts a positive charge by subsuming them to the greater mystery of the supernatural. In a sense, the mystery *is* the explanation: the soul is explained by God, and God is beyond human comprehension (for example). Outside such a context, the idea of something being meaningfully unexplained becomes far less stable, but still a term like 'humanity' that might be used as a secular alternative to 'soul' is in all important respects no less impenetrable.

What does it mean to praise a person or a work of art as 'very human'? Francis Fukuyama points out in *Our Posthuman Future* (2002) that the concept of humanity (as a virtue) depends on the idea that we are born with an unfathomable aspect of ourselves, a deep what-it-is-like to be us that we cannot properly explain. It is not as though religiousness solves this inexplicability, or provides the correct way of thinking about it, but it does at least give it formal acknowledgment, and codifies it, and thereby creates context for it. Institutional religion is buttressed by an inheritance of tradition and ritual, forms of living – services, actions, customs – that embody the ideology (literally 'bring it to life'). This is one reason why religion might command respect compared to the person who asserts they *just know* that there's something more out there' (whatever that means), or *just know* that there is such a thing as a soul' (whatever that is), whilst carrying on in all other aspects like someone who believes no such thing. Their attitude makes no difference.

Today, we could say of the loss of cultural authority, the formal difficulties, the slowing of innovation to a crawl – none of it would matter tremendously if there were a core, immutable good that literature continued to provide. In fact, without all that old momentum it becomes, if anything, even easier to feel that literature serves no profound purpose. The private belief that there is something intrinsically valuable in art owes more than it appears to consensus. Hemmingway was not wrong to say that writing has something inexplicable about it, but he spoke from a position of strength. The 1952 publication of *The Old Man and the Sea* was an American national event. Hemmingway could rely on a context for his work. The disorientation of the modern writer is very much an absence of context, a loss detectable even in the words we use to try and highlight the special value of literature. It seems to me that one perfectly understandable response to this is to declare that there is no such value, and never was: a retreat into depressive realism. 'Books are a load of crap.' One notably persistent theme in Houellebecq's novels is the contempt given over to imaginative and intellectual life – the formal self-disgust. Recall the dismissal that begins *H.P. Lovecraft*: 'It is useless… to write new realistic novels. We generally know where we stand in relation to reality and don't care to know any more.' *Whatever* describes literature as 'pure bullshit'. In *Atomised* writing is called a displacement activity, the performance of frustrated animals. When Bruno recounts his time teaching literature to sixteen-year-olds, he lashes out at his memory of one of the black students: 'He always wore a baseball cap and a pair of Nikes; I was convinced he had a huge dick. All the girls threw themselves at this big baboon and here I was trying to teach them about Mallarmé – what the fuck was the point?' The hero of *Platform*, Michel R., informs us that 'My conclusion… is that art cannot change lives. At least not mine.' According to Daniel in *The Possibility of an Island*, 'After a certain age… it's quite obvious that *everything has been said and done*', theorising is good only after sex – i.e. 'real life':

> I had probably never had a real conversation with anyone other than a woman I loved, and essentially it seemed unsurprising to me that the exchange of ideas with someone who doesn't know your body, is not in a position to secure its unhappiness or on the other hand to bring it joy, was a false and ultimately impossible exercise, for we are bodies, we are, above all, principally and almost uniquely bodies, and the state of our bodies constitutes the true explanation of the majority of our intellectual and moral conceptions.

The disrespect for intellectual and artistic activity dovetails with the novels' obsession with inner drives, and the futility of awareness in the face of bodily urge. Michel R. reflects at one point that 'there's probably no point searching for meaning' in his personality, it's 'just a technical matter, a question of hormone levels'. This is a characteristic moment of depressive realism: whether or not we understand ourselves, it makes no great difference. In *Platform*, Michel R. arrives in a Thai brothel, chancing across two other men from his package tour. One of these men, Robert, is a weary cynic. The scene is fascinating because the narrator's judgment can so easily be interpreted as Houellebecq's own, upon himself:

> I nodded to Robert to take my leave. His dour face, fixed in a bitter rictus, scanned the room – and beyond, the human race – without a hint of affability. He had made his point, at least he had had the opportunity; I sensed I was going to forget him pretty quickly. I had the impression that he didn't even want to make love to these girls anymore. Life can be seen as a process of gradually coming to a standstill... In Robert, the process was already well advanced: he possibly still got erections, but even that wasn't certain. It's easy to play the smart aleck, to give the impression that you've understood something about life; the fact remains that life comes to an end. My fate was similar to his, we had shared the same defeat; but still I felt no active sense of solidarity. In the absence of love, nothing can be sanctified. On the inside of the eyelids patches of light merge; there are visions, there are dreams. None of this now concerns man, who waits for night; night comes. I paid the waiter two thousand baht and he escorted me to the double doors leading upstairs. [The girl] held my hand; she would, for an hour or two, try to make me happy.

\*\*\*

Something that David Foster Wallace made much of in his work was the idea that literature served as a comfort to loneliness, and that this was maybe its most basic virtue. If you accept that loneliness is the great existential terror that we all, in our different ways, try to escape, it isn't hard to apprehend the fraught relationship that this gives us to our own bodies, because it's our bodies that keep us so basically and dreadfully apart. It's interesting to note how often words used to express the value of literature (or art more generally) conjure up kinds of immaterialism: 'seeing the world through different eyes', 'being transported', forging a 'psychic connection' with the author, 'losing yourself' in a book – all of these are expressions that run against what seems to be the brute material truth: that we are locked inside our skulls. Nor is it a great challenge to draw connections between this and the spiritual immaterialism inherent in religion (think about the phrase 'Giving yourself to God'). Partly, these ways of speaking may be extensions of a vague but deep-rooted sense that what is distinctive and important about being human are things that find their best expression in non-biological, non-material terms, like when someone says that intimacy is the genuinely valuable part of sex. (Here is the reason we cling on to words like 'soul'.) The villainy of materialism is that it undermines this: for instance, when it tells us that love is only a disguise for the urge to reproduce. Along this road we lose the use of a very fundamental and comforting terminology, or at least are obliged to admit that it gives a false or misleading account of human behaviour. It emerges that there is basically no getting over yourself, no escaping your skull – and the more you are led to feel this way the more you are inclined to see life as isolated and vanishing.

Houellebecq's men don't think about God. All they think about – all there is – are the dictates of their biology, and their diminishing capacities to meet them. It is as if to say: the facts are what they are. So long as the facts are in your favour you can be happy, but there's nothing else to it. Not only is this position terribly lonely, it ridicules concepts of the common good. When

Immanuel Kant argued that God must be judged by the same morality as men he was saying, partly, that what is truly good must be as eternal and universal as God himself, because if the good is only open to some – if it is dependent in any way on luck, for example – then it cannot really *be* good, since its contingency would be an evil. A value-system like the value-system of a hedonist, which relies entirely on the working of the body, is akin to the kind of contingent-good that Kant thought couldn't possibly be the real thing, i.e. it is good only for whoever it is good for. So sexual freedom is a boon *if* you are able to enjoy it, but that 'if' carries with it the reality of all those people, the Raphaël Tisserands, who are left out. The picture Houellebecq paints across the nightclubs, resorts and restaurants of the West is of a society that understands the facts but won't spell them out, where concern for the body (health, beauty, sensation) has been raised to a cultural zenith, only without any corresponding apparatus to give meaning to decline and death. This, he opines, is the bleak consequence of consumer capitalism, 'which, turning youth into the supremely desirable commodity, had little by little destroyed respect for tradition and the cult of the ancestors – inasmuch as it promised the indefinite preservation of this same youth, and the pleasures associated with it'.

Modern materialism has this strange kind of double-effect on self-perception. On the one hand, it isolates the individual by (seemingly) dispelling various illusions of communion (the decline of religion being the paradigm example). On the other, progress in social sciences, psychology and neurology encourages us to think about ourselves in various external fashions: as the product of genetic resources, social and economic starting position, and so on. These modes of thought are uncomfortable because they imply that our view of things 'from the inside' is illusory or distorted, and that what we experience as central and singular in our personal day-to-day lives are actually nothing more than instances of general truths about human behaviour. To a certain extent it is healthy to be objective about yourself, but at its limits it becomes dehumanising. 'Flattening' is, for me, exactly the word for describing how the materialist double-effect feels when you reach these limits – subjective consciousness is squished between the material barrier separating our inner life from those of others, and the inferential awareness that this inner life is itself the product of a hard-wiring that we are subjectively blind to. The deeper way in which Sontag was right when she said that redundancy was the affliction of modern life is that the ascendancy of materialism not only attacks the meaning of this very precious 'immaterial' vocabulary we use to talk about what it's like being human, it breeds biological fatalism, lending weight to the idea that our actions reduce to, and are determined by, dumb physical process, an ultimately pointless set of natural drives. Helplessness is the current running beneath all of Houellebecq's narratives, the inability to either get what you want or change what you want; to avoid death or believe that death is anything except bad.

This is the omega point of depressive realism. What good are books if you are sick, alone, and unloved? They are no good. At best they are make-believe to help us disguise the facts of life – but the facts remain, and they are unbearably heavy. Hence the dark joke at the bottom of the pessimist's project is that it subverts itself. Ridiculing the futility of human action finally makes pessimism seem pointless, demonstrates the emptiness of its honesty. Depressive realism leads us up to an airless summit, and the wonder is how seriously we can take it; whether, despite itself, there is anything to be drawn from its negativity.

3

## Your Imagination is a Liar

You don't have to think very hard to realize that our dread of both relationships and loneliness, both of which are like sub-dreads of our dread of being trapped inside a self (a psychic self, not just a physical self), has to do with angst about death, the recognition that I'm going to die, and die very much alone, and the rest of the world is going to go merrily on without me. I'm not sure I could give you a steeple-fingered theoretical justification, but I strongly suspect a big part of real art fiction's job is to aggravate this sense of entrapment and loneliness and death in people, to move people to countenance it, since any possible human redemption requires us first to face what's dreadful, what we want to deny.

*David Foster Wallace*

The fundamental inconsistency in depressive realism was reached at the end of the last chapter: if you follow the pessimist's logic to its conclusion, it collapses under its own weight. Its 'truthfulness' makes truth-telling seem pointless. Houellebecq's fiction, like all depressive realism, trades heavily on its guise of honesty, and here the tight resemblance between Houellebecq the real-life man and the protagonists in his novels serves artistic purpose, insofar as it reinforces the impression of undiluted (or less-diluted) candour. But the appearance of undiluted honesty should never be trusted, and the simple physical existence of pessimistic art subverts its philosophy. Whether the pessimist's work rubbishes the value of art explicitly, as Houellebecq's does, or merely implies it through its worldview – still the pessimist's work is also art, and it exists. What for? It would be less important if there were no claims to consistency being made, but the lure of depressive realism is precisely that it presents an unvarnished, 'completed' picture of the world. Notoriously, depressive thinking is characterised by certainty. Its dissonances matter.

George Orwell said that inconsistency can be a mark of vitality, and this seems doubly apt when the inconsistency lies within an ethos preaching disgust and hatred at life. The issue is not bad faith, as if what the pessimist writes is false and he knows it. It's that, whatever he thinks about it, the very fact of his writing suggests something left unsettled. Ironically, depressive realism – which regards itself as the most clear-headed, disillusioned, unclouded way of perceiving the world – doesn't know how to explain itself. Where would the force of Houellebecq's novels come from, if art has no power? To respond that art is just a trumped up way of achieving some 'lower' goal (e.g. that Houellebecq writes books in order to make himself seem important or attractive) still doesn't explain how it works. What is it that makes a particular book good? What attracts someone to one piece of art but not another?

But just that Houellebecq's books have blind-spots and inconsistencies isn't proof that what they say is wrong, only an invitation to consider how it's not completely right. It is no coincidence, thought, that the moment at which depressive realist art goes blind is over its own status as art, i.e. its identity as an 'unreal', imagined thing – artifice. Every kind of art is unreal after a fashion, but the point is particularly obvious with respect to literature. Fiction is fiction no matter how realistically it is written (the characters aren't real people; the tables and chairs aren't real tables and chairs, etc.). So with any sort of literary realism there's a certain degree of ambiguity about what's being asserted. By its nature, realism is a state of opposition – it only makes sense in contrast with what's unreal: fantasy, illusion, myth, lies, and so on. But thought of as a literary virtue, 'realism' therefore seems strictly incoherent or impossible or both, because how can fiction ever be real? It's an age-old question, and, again, the core tension of the discipline may really be as basic as this: the need for fiction to be (somehow) real and have (somehow) a real worth, versus its inability to be anything less than fake. Admittedly, the terms 'real' and 'fake' are awfully simplistic, but they are extraordinarily hard to see beyond. Even very sophisticated theories about the inadequacy of sorting anything, and not just art, into clumsy categories of right and wrong (or true and false, real and fake) are bedevilled by the purity of the terms they try to oppose. It is fiendishly difficult to escape these first ways of thinking, inadequate as they may be.

Sontag wrote that our ingrained disposition to think of art as a matter of mimesis or representation (and therefore as something at a remove from reality, fake) is the reason we are stuck defending it until the end of consciousness. There is a gravity-like tendency within the intellect to belittle art, to see it as an embellishment or a bauble on existence, rather than anything vital. It's one of the critic's jobs to try and find ways of suspending this instinct. The challenge is to remain sensitive to how culture shifts, making some methods of defence redundant and creating the need for new ones, and it has to be performed in the knowledge that there's no sure ground to find. It's never a question of *proving* that art is worthwhile, which is impossible, but the fuzzier and more ill-defined issue of how plausible the *belief* that art is worthwhile can be made. Given the problems of self-reference that depressive realist art falls into, it seems to me that one good way to detect cracks in depressive realist philosophy might be to think more about why art is a valuable thing. But of course the question is muddled when depressive realism itself produces compelling works of art. The dissonance between Houellebecq's attack on 'realistic novels' at the start of *H.P. Lovecraft* and his own flatly realist prose; the divide between his novels' form and their content; the egotism of his characters versus their transparent self-disgust – all of it indicates something about the limits of his type of realism. Yet it doesn't cancel the force of his books. So a good question to begin with would be: how is it even possible that art breathing contempt for itself can manage to seem righter, truer, and more urgent than art that does not? And what is it about our time and place that encourages this?

*\*\*\**

Among the gifts possessed by the late David Foster Wallace was a genius for talking about writing, a talent that allowed him to perform exceptionally well in a role I suppose authors now find it difficult to avoid, that of the apologist/justifier/defender to literature's continued existence. In an interview on Michael Silverblatt's Bookworm radio show in 2006, Wallace gave a good account of the challenge a modern artist faces unpicking her voice from the culture at large:

> it seems to me, having been born in 1962, and having grown up without any memory of a life without television, for example, is that in fact what we have when you talk about stuff like the ethical or moral dimensions to art, is we really have what appear to me to be two different problems who are related in complicated ways. One is the classic one of just deciding (the writer decides the way that all of us have to decide): what is it to be a human being? To find some way to make an accommodation with being an individual and being self-centred, but also being part of a larger group, and loving some people, all that stuff. But then the other concerns appear to me to be more rhetorical or technical. Something that doesn't get talked about very much in any era I know of up 'til maybe the postmodern, is that these are also public

documents and works of art that are not meant simply to be expressive, that are not meant simply to be spontaneous effusions from an individual soul, they are also communications and pieces of art that are designed to please, gratify, edify, whatever, other human beings. So that you've got not just what's true for me as a person, but what's going to *sound* true? What's going to hit readers, or music listeners, or whatever; what's going to hit their nerve-endings as true in 2006, or 2000, or 1995? And it seems to me (I may have a kind of pessimistic view of it) that the situation, the environment, in which nervous systems receive these communications is vastly more complicated, difficult, cynical and over-hyped than it used to be. The easy example is that, and one that I go through over and over with students in writing classes, is that these students are far more afraid of coming off as sentimental than they are of coming off twisted, obscene, gross, any of the things that used to be the really horrible things that you didn't want to betray about yourself. The great danger of appearing sentimental is that sentimentality is mainly now used in what appear to be very cynical marketing or mass-entertainment devices that are meant to sort of manhandle the emotions of large numbers of people who aren't paying very close attention. So that some of the most urgent themes, or issues – how to deal with mourning the loss of someone you love very much? – have been so adulterated by sort of treacly, cynical, commercial art that it becomes very, very, very difficult to think about how to talk about it in a way that's not just more of that crap.

The contempt for art in Houellebecq's novels is more than just an interesting logical inconsistency (how can art be anti-art?), it's also part of what makes the books so pertinent. In lots of ways, cynicism (and by extension, pessimism) about art is not only very easy now, it's *reasonable*. Some of the causes of this are relatively shallow, and some are deeply serious and complicated, but they all bend back to the elemental difficulty of finding justifications for art. But then again, isn't it basically superfluous to ask for a good reason for art to exist? Evidently people go on being creative and enjoying art without having well worked-out theories about why they do so, and you'd be hard pressed to deny that whatever the mechanisms of creation and aesthetic enjoyment are, they run deeper than conscious rationale. Indeed, theoretical justifications for art tend to look silly or pretentious, sooner or later, because they intellectualise what seems instinctive (possibility this is a mark of philosophy in general). What could be more natural – more human – than creativity? But, as Wallace says, one of the real difficulties at the moment is that we're given so many good reasons to be guarded and self-conscious and generally wary of our instincts when it comes to aesthetics. This is a trouble every sort of art faces, although perhaps it's easier to appreciate in literature, since fiction is already so naturally inclined towards self-consciousness and doubt.

What is it about the world today that makes justifying art harder than it might be? Keep literature as our example. As well as the issues described in the last chapter (of scale and fit) there is a more insidious third trouble for writers, or rather a nest of closely-related troubles, to do with the saturation of culture. Novelists encounter a world not only overloaded with information but overloaded with novels, possibly overloaded with novels confronting the overload of information. On an immediate social level, the enormity of published work has the effect of isolating readers. The general dispersal of culture into fragmented and miscellaneous units in the information-age has a more pronounced effect on literature, if only because novels typically take longer to read than films take to watch or albums take to listen to. It takes comparatively more effort to know about the same things, therefore it's less common. The upshot is that it is more difficult to get the kind of basic social-reinforcement around literature that merges individual interests into a scene or community that people want to belong to, which is one of the main reasons it's now such a challenge for writers to fix co-ordinates for their work. The mass of already-existing fiction feeds back into the process of writing in other ways, too. For a start, it stresses the importance of relevance and engagement – because if all the reader wants is 'a good read' there is already enough unsurpassable writing to fill up lifetime upon lifetime. But the difficulty is that being relevant and engaged would seem to require some minimum level of (rather unforgiving) self-consciousness, since one of the big informing worries of a working novelist has to be that there is already far too much to read. Really, it's the problem for art since modernism began: because the world has a superabundance of art, art with designs on relevance is under tremendous pressure to take this super-abundance as its subject. Except this results in predictable loops of anxiety and self-consciousness, since if the topic to engage with is the overdose of information and fantasy, how can adding *more* information and fantasy (in the form of art) possibly help?

Connected to this – and what's maybe the most dispiriting problem of all for an artist trying to justify herself – is the peculiarly insulating effect that cultural overload has on our aesthetic perceptions. Like a lot of the phenomena associated with the term 'postmodernism' the causes and effects of this insulation seem very diffuse and hard to put into words, but one fairly straightforward example of what I mean is the clash between *life as art presents it* and *life as it is experienced*. Typically (in the course of twelve episodes, or one hundred and twenty minutes running-time, or three-hundred pages, or whatever) narrative art gives us images of lives more vividly felt and wholly eventful than our own. There's nothing sinister about this. Dramatic compression is a practical necessity – audiences won't usually allow themselves to be bored. It's just that the more of this colourful stuff you take in, the harder it is to avoid the thought of how relatively mundane and colourless your own existence is compared to all these interesting people onscreen and on-page. I doubt this idea, even should it occur, is the cause of too much grief for the average well-adjusted adult, because after all it's just books/movies/TV shows we're talking about, there's no need to take them seriously as ideals for living. For an artist or for someone wondering about why art is worthwhile, however, this sensible qualifier tumbles into a more worrying question: how, then, *should* narrative art be taken seriously? Or must it always be kept at an ego-preserving distance? What makes it more than just an aesthetic concern is the fact that narrative art (of any variety) transmits not only entertainment, but also values. Stories send messages about the goodness of love and the badness of evil and everything in between. They provide models of behaviour for us to evaluate. All this is obvious enough, and equally obvious is that to become numb toward stories is to risk becoming numb to their attendant questions of value. Saturation creates a type of 'aesthetic filter' in the consciousness, a thickened awareness of how, for example, grief is transformed (through performance and repetition) into 'grief', love into 'love'; how, as the world becomes more dense with cultural product, real life seems to somehow absorb the character of a staged fake.[5] Which sets up a punishing formal obstacle for artists and critics: how to preserve the notion that art is a channel for genuine, informative, life-defining values and principles, whilst protecting said values from the tranquilising effect of art in a culture overdosing on aesthetics?

This dilemma, left untreated, ends up generating huge amounts of disappointment and cynicism (essentially just disappointment, fortified) in artist and audience alike. It simply becomes harder to trust the messages art sends, which then leads directly into all those unpleasant, endless misgivings about whether art can *ever* be trusted, given that artwork is always manipulative and false to some extent. Consider the distinction between commercial and non-commercial art Wallace alludes to in the interview quoted above. One interesting aspect about the treacly, manhandling sorts of art that he mentions is that being able to recognise their tricks is frequently no defence against them. The swelling string music at the climactic moment in a movie, the soaring key change in a song – it's easy to feel yourself bullied into an emotional response even when you know perfectly well how mawkish and manipulative the thing you're responding to is. This reaction is actually double-faceted: on a first-level, there is the quasi-forced emoting, and, on a second, resentment; both at the art for manipulating you and at yourself for being so open to manipulation. (Isn't something very similar often true of advertising – an initial, impulsive desire for the idealised situation or person on show, which is hard to eradicate precisely because it is unconsidered, or rather, pre-considered?) The natural defence-mechanism against this is cynicism. You protect your integrity by assuming an intellectual distance from your immediate emotional reaction. For the artist, though – supposing the artist wants to make her audience emote, but in a way that is somehow more sincere and serious than commercial art – the problem becomes how to go beyond the 'soft-spots' that commerce so ruthlessly homes in on. This is difficult, firstly, because the reason commercial art is made to zero in on these triggers is that they *work*, powerfully and indiscriminately, that's how money gets made. So it seems as though the artist has to strike some balance between finding effective ways to inspire a response and foregoing the reliable techniques that commercial art uses, lest their work become just more of the very treacly, manipulative pap that makes people so cynical. Achieving that balance is tricky enough, but then the next thing all of this does is induce another dose of malignant self-consciousness. Because it might easily occur to the artist that once an element of cunning is introduced to the work, once you start thinking about the best way to go about that work if you want people to think of you as genuine and not cheap, you're already failing. Naturally you want to seem like you're working from the heart. However, *seeming* sincere is crucially removed from *being* sincere – certainly if it's you doing the seeming, you thinking about the best way to seem, then it begins to exhibit an awful lot of the hallmarks of lying. In which case, what makes the artist's work more virtuous than the commercial stuff they don't want to be mixed up with? It's a problem Wallace illustrated by way of the old televisual oxymoron of 'acting natural'. The very best actors work as if the camera isn't there, but of course there's nothing natural about it. It's an incredibly sophisticated, considered, and difficult-to-do masquerade. Being (actually) natural on camera is hopeless. Without training people freeze up, speak haltingly and generally look extremely stupid – and so faking is necessary to make any positive impression at all. As such, the worry about how to separate oneself from disingenuous culture can wind up producing even more cynicism about the possibility of being artistically honest, authentic, and non-fake.

At one point in *Atomised*, Michel Djerzinski muses: 'A lie is useful if it transforms reality... but if it fails, then all that's left is the lie, the bitterness and knowledge that it was a lie.' It's not art he has in mind, but the analogy is easy enough. The fraudulence of literature, say, could be ignored so long as you felt it possessed transformational power, either outwardly (to cause social change) or inwardly (to enrich the soul). But if these hopes are dismissed – because a novel won't ever change the world, because there is no soul to enrich – then the question is: what's left? The most obvious answer is 'pleasure'. But this response isn't as straightforward as it looks. No one would deny that art's capacity to give pleasure is fundamental to its appeal, yet although pleasure is perfectly innocent in some circumstances, in others it can be demeaning, self-indulgent and hollow. In which case, what is it that separates 'good' pleasure from 'bad' pleasure? As Houellebecq might put it, not only is aesthetic enjoyment (in general) pathetically faint compared to the force of other, more basic appetites, *anything* valued solely in terms of individual enjoyment is logically self-absorbed. So for art to be more than a narcissistic exercise the issue can't be simply whether or not it pleases, but also to what end it pleases, and how well – which casts us back into the problem of what, if anything, guarantees worth. Wallace described late-twentieth century America as a 'confusion of permissions', which applies. Technically, art has the freedom to be 'for' almost anything the artist likes (I can write this novel in favour of murder, you can paint a picture for political reform) but even these agendas take on the feel of superficial gestures, none more particularly serious than others. Artists become 'artists'; their messages become 'messages', drained of substance.

Once again, the broad result of this is more disappointment, disenchantment and cynicism – none of which ultimately helps anybody. The only piece of long-form literary theory Wallace ever published, the essay 'E Unibus Pluram: Television and U.S. Fiction', took the history of post-war, postmodernist American literature as a case study in the poisonous effects self-consciousness cynicism had on art. From the 1950s onwards a family of American authors – including William Burroughs, John Barth, Robert Coover and Thomas Pynchon, among others – were united (whatever their differences) by the use of cynicism, irony and irreverence as tools to expose the distance they perceived between the myths of the American Dream and the realities of consumer capitalism; all the assorted big and little hypocrisies of American self-image. This sort of postmodernist fiction could be crudely defined as a marriage of the old modernist credo of formal innovation to pop-culture and mass-image, plus a certain learned irony (inherited from modernism, but exaggerated) toward its own status as literary fiction. The aesthetic shift into postmodernism parallels a moral shift into myth-busting: just as artists became more focused on exposing fakery in the culture at large, it was only consistent that they took more of an interest in the artifice of their own work. Fiction arrived loaded with non-linear plots, transgressive characters, topical references and allusions to mass-culture, so too waves of fiction about writers writing fiction; fiction commenting on its own fictitiousness; fiction employing 'fourth-wall' busting appeals to the reader (the title story in Barth's *Lost in the Funhouse* (1968) is exemplary), in short, a lot of fiction that pin-wheeled its arms about how artificial everything was, up to and including literary fiction, in the post-atomic American experience. This aesthetic pretty clearly evolved, Wallace argued, 'as an intellectual expression of the "rebellious youth culture" of the '60s and '70s' – and so its eventual co-option into mainstream culture is roughly analogous to that of rock music, another example of how exciting countercultural trends can become tamed habits of consumption. Writing in 1990, Wallace identified the cutting-edge of postmodernist literature with a genre he called 'Image-Fiction': a kind of hyper-speed pastiche that mimicked the flutter of television, giving inner lives to Barbie-dolls, Walkmans, public figures and TV personalities; using 'the transient received myths of popular culture as a *world* in which to imagine fictions about "real," albeit pop-mediated characters'. The aesthetic of Image-Fiction might have been more heavily immersed in mass-media, but the moral was still essentially that of postmodernist satire: to put the absurdities of modern America on show, to call attention to the power and extent of the hold of fantasy on popular imagination. The catch was that while Image-Fiction writers were correct to regard television (which Wallace used as a litmus for mass-culture) as the single greatest common denominator and sensibility-shaper in America, they missed the fact that by the mid-1980s TV had assimilated irreverence and ridicule so successfully into itself that, although parodies to the effect that popular culture was cynical, absurd, artificial, etc. might have been right on, they also became totally ineffective. Subversion reaches a dead-end once the prevailing cultural values *are* values of mockery, where mass culture is complicit with 'high-brow' counterculture in irony and trivialisation. A great example of this in practice is the weird idol-worship/mob-lynching contortions of the celebrity-press. (It's not a joke when someone says that celebrity culture is beyond parody. How would you make fun of it? For being shallow, narcissistic, capricious, dumb? It isn't from thinking it's profound that people take an interest.) Far from shaking us out of our illusions, at this point satire ends up bizarrely reinforcing the status quo. So long as we can tell ourselves we don't take it seriously, it's okay to stay tuned.

'What do you do when postmodern rebellion becomes a pop-cultural institution?' asked Wallace. His worry was over the neutralisation of one kind of rebel-art, but with the benefit of hindsight we can identify it as part of a much wider cultural trend, a process cultural theorist Mark Fisher, in *Capitalist Realism* (2009), termed *precorporation*: the apparent transformation of every gesture and meta-gesture into market-tested cliché: 'the pre-emptive formatting and shaping of desires, aspirations and hopes by capitalist culture'. A state with a lack of breathing space, where the desire for authenticity has been so well-identified it becomes smothered. In the face of this, unchecked cynicism is worse than useless – it pacifies; as though the mere awareness of being ill could be substituted for a cure. A great deal of what Wallace said about writing in interviews revolved around the importance of rehabilitating 'simple' values in art,[6] but, as he alluded to at the end of 'E Unibus Pluram', the basic challenge is not to renounce cynicism in favour of earnestness, but to appreciate how the present situation might require postmodernist techniques at the same time as it desperately needs to transcend them, i.e. to find a way to be earnest and sentimental while keeping one's eyes open to the conditions that give rise to cynicism and irony, which after all didn't come out of a vacuum.[7]

\*\*\*

Decades on from a seismic shift in the public's perception of how art is meant to work – the 'transition from art's being a creative instantiation of real values to art's being a creative rejection of bogus values', in Wallace's words – there's self-evidently still no shortage of fake, hypocritical, trashy culture to oppose. The underbelly of consumer capitalism is not something hidden. And yet the durability of a culture that panders to self-centredness isn't hard to fathom either, since, to say nothing else, it has one singular phenomenological fact on its side – the unshakable illusion possessed by everyone that they are each at the very centre of creation, alone. Fiction with a nihilist bent is (in one way) just a natural progression from postmodernist satire, pitting itself against everything except, finally, what appears undeniable: basic instincts, and the isolation of the self. Instead of any high-flown 'making strange', Houellebecq tries to make the reader feel the way they do already, only much worse. It's not that all his theories are plausible. The ambience of his books is what really tells – their dull, bone-deep bitterness. Taking it as axiomatic that there's a current of frustrated desire Western culture feeds on and intensifies, Houellebecq ramps up the resentment – at the failure of life to live up to its billing; at the distance between virtual attractions and everyday landfill; at the creeping feeling that there's a gigantic party going on all the time somewhere that you haven't been invited to; at a cultural nervous system toxified by wanting and not having, having and not wanting anymore; and at all (to quote Wallace once again) 'the really rather brilliantly managed stress everybody is made to feel about staying fit and looking good and living long and squeezing the absolute maximum productivity and health and self-actuation out of every last vanishing second'. Instead of trying to fight past cynicism and weariness, Houellebecq conducts energy straight through them. The most forceful moments are always the most certain. The moral is always *you know this all already*.

But Houellebecq's books aren't as self-assured as they seem, and this returns to the blind-spot that depressive realist art has about itself. If what the characters in Houellebecq say is true, it seems to cancel the art's reason to be; but it's the author's skill, his art, that makes them sound true. If their solipsism and self-interest are compelling, it's only because the reader can sympathise. It's an inconsistency exhibited within the novels, too, filled up as they are with characters who constantly assert the uselessness of writing but who keep on producing it themselves. The narrator of *Whatever* writes philosophical parables. Bruno composes essays and poems. Michel Djerzinski completes a book of philosophy. Daniel writes love poetry. Near the end of both *Platform* and *The Possibility of an Island* the narrative is revealed to have been a written memoir. *Atomised*, too, turns out to be a composition – the story has been written by a neo-human. Acts of writing, as much as the disgust for writing, are everywhere in Houellebecq's fiction. It's interesting that almost the last thing Daniel does before he dies is send Esther dozens of useless letters, trying to win her back. A different character (commenting on Daniel's life story) describes it as 'a last and pathetic attempt to deny reality... this love without end he speaks of existed only in his imagination'. There is something microcosmic about this: an ineffectual message written in the name of an imaginary ideal, a compulsive attempt to deny reality.

The rhetorical self-harm in Houellebecq's novels is an example of depressive realism struggling with its own contradictions and impossibilities. In some respects, not only are Houellebecq's novels unimaginative (in their reductive worldview), they are *anti*-imaginative too; they actively dislike the imagination. Houellebecq hammers the mantra that the engine of consumer capitalism is a terrible intensification of desire, which makes satisfaction progressively harder. He means sex, but the idea might just as well be generalised. What's significant is its defeatism. The thought that one is enslaved by desire even in the knowledge that it's harmful; left in thrall to the rampaging power of idiotic urges (as if to say: 'This is what I want, whether or not I like it!'). A confusion specific to Houellebecq, rather than depressive realism in general, is that his novels capitulate to fantasy, over and over again; the same fantasies they blame human suffering on. This is the weird naivety that springs up in every one of his books, with the exception of *Whatever* – the moments when cynical realism seemingly dissolves into fantasy, be it sentimental love or (more usually) pornographic bliss. You get the impression that Houellebecq realises how incredible these events are, since he always returns to sabotage them afterwards, to denounce them as false promises. Nonetheless, the novels they belong to would not work if they were removed. Without the unnaturally perfect lovers in *Platform*, *The Possibility of an Island* and *La Carte et le Territoire* there would be no plot. *Atomised* pivots on a dreamlike sex scene that sets up the second half of the story. In the Nietzschian sense, Houellebecq's books are decadent: in love with what is harmful. His 'realism' is fundamentally split, with cynicism on one side, and intoxication with realer-than-real fantasies on the other. But rather than giving to lie to his worldview, it is this split, this incompatibility, which attaches him so well to his time and place.

The greatest strength of consumerism (and also it's most unhappy aspect) is that it exists only with our complicity. There is a level at which the depthless fantasies it presents simply *are* what we want. Some good examples of this are the eternally-returning stories in certain parts of the media about the neuroses given to average women from a fashion industry constantly bombarding them with injunctions to be thinner, younger and more perfect. It would seem beyond doubt that the worries are justified, i.e. that fashion images really do set unattainable, anxiety-inducing norms. So why do the objections feel so feeble? Why does nothing ever change? What's problematic about condemning the fashion industry for being unrealistic is that it never aspires to be realistic in the first place; indeed it lives off our own *un*reasonable desires. (The point is even more obvious now that pictures of models are digitally 'enhanced' as a matter of course. It is literally impossible for someone to look this way, but that's what sells.) Consciously or not, Houellebecq's writing exhibits the schizophrenic pull of consumption culture – how unreal it seems, and yet how enmeshed in it we remain. And one reason it's so hard for art to exercise a grip on the modern psyche is that, in a way, consumerism has already turned our imagination against us, and taught us to distrust it. It's interesting that whenever Houellebecq describes happiness it is, almost invariably, as a blankness. The orgasms that obliterate self-consciousness; or the passage in *Platform* when Michel R. recalls his brief, contented time with his lover, 'of which, paradoxically, I have so few memories'; even the utopia at the end of *Atomised*, referred to rather than described. Within their medium, the novels seem to find happiness unimaginable. Instead the imagination is the enemy, a liar – the ultimate faker. There's a saying that misanthropy is always a disguised form of self-contempt, which, in this case, is perfectly correct. Houellebecq's books are works of the imagination against the imagination. They hate themselves.

## 4

# Everything and Nothing

Clinical depression resembles a malign, lived paradox. The irreconcilability is between the all-consuming world the disease creates for the depressive – the inability to perceive any separate other – and the apprehension that this *everything* is also *nothing*, that the world has no 'real', positive content or worth. In the same way that depressive realist art is unable explain its own existence, the depressed person cannot accept hers, and this failure of processing is agony. In his novel *Infinite Jest* (1996), Wallace described psychotic depression as 'probably mostly indescribable except as a sort of double bind in which any/all of the alternatives we associate with human agency – sitting or standing, doing or resting, speaking or keeping silent, living or dying – are not just unpleasant but literally horrible. It is also lonely on a level that cannot be conveyed.' Depression is the pathological frontier of individualism – the point at which the whole world is eaten up by the self.

The dissonance between all-important and not-important in clinical depression (its supreme but also worthless loneliness) is the background mood of Houellebecq's novels, and it is a key to many of the aesthetic and ethical problems they distil. Whatever else you think of him, it's hard to fault Houellebecq for his ambition. He certainly doesn't shy away from the most fundamental themes of love, loss, death and so forth. So it's striking that this seriousness of purpose also correlates with a kind of self-negation, a total unseriousness. Not only is it hard to understand what good it possibly does, if we're taking the novels at their word, to see the universe in such a merciless fashion, there's also the performative contradiction of depressive realist art, and beyond that the simple *pettiness* of so much of Houellebecq's philosophy. Is it really the most significant thing – not getting enough sex and being angry about it?

But there are real, macro-scale phenomena behind the reductive individualism Houellebecq peddles. Jean-François Lyotard described the postmodern era as the end of 'metanarratives', a judgment that's been debated, but which is true insofar as it spells out the logical consequence for fiction-writing in a world grown too broad and various for literature. To borrow Fredric Jameson's term, novelists seem unable to 'totalise' the world any longer: the big story, such as it is, isn't one they are equipped for. But this is true largely because the big story isn't one that *anybody* is equipped for. In his essay 'Cognitive Mapping' (1988), Jameson noted how personal experience is an increasingly unreliable guide to the truth of our time and place, given that everyday reality is now entwined with bewilderingly huge systems of finance and information, and crucial first-hand realities – the price of goods, for example – are set in place by forces almost completely beyond first-hand awareness. In these conditions, wrote Jameson, 'the phenomenological experience of the individual subject, traditionally the supreme raw materials of the work of art, becomes limited to a tiny corner of the social world, a fixed camera view of a certain section of London or the countryside or whatever. But the truth of that experience no longer coincides with the place in which it takes place. The truth of that limited daily experience of London lies, rather, in India or Jamaica or Hong Kong...' It's not only the defining conflicts of the era (the War on Terror, climate change, etc.) that are difficult to appreciate from ground-level in the West. Even our limited, daily, ground-level experience is shaped by almost unfathomably complex, man-made networks of capital and exchange, the structural coordinates of which 'are no longer accessible to immediate lived experience and... often not even conceptualizable for most people'.

Which is to say, although the workings of the world – the reasons how and why our society is arranged the way it is – could perhaps be represented using scientific or mathematical models, there is no non-abstract way of seeing for yourself where the explanation lies. 'There comes into being, then,' continued Jameson, 'a situation in which we can say that if individual experience is authentic, then it cannot be true; and that if a scientific or cognitive model of the same content is true, then it escapes individual experience. It is evident that this new situation poses tremendous and crippling problems for a work of art.' That it does, but even before that it places a huge burden on any individual's sense of identity. When Bruno declares, in *Atomised*, that the modern world reduces a man 'to the sum of his own experience', it's more than just an excuse for self-indulgence. The difficulty of relating local experience to any social totality tends to reduce identity to personalised anchors: the everyday work you do, your friends, family, close community, etc. It's not that we have no stories to tell, but that our stories have fallen drastically out of synch with the processes making the world what it is.

A well-known irony of globalisation is that the incredible expanse of activity and interconnection it reveals to us inspires nothing, on a personal level, so much as feelings of isolation, impotence and insignificance. But then again, in another way, it also makes everyday problems feel like the only *real* problems there are, being the only issues we experience directly or exercise any real degree of control over. You end up with the weird feeling that your own private concerns are both *the most important things* and *not important at all* – an echo of the clinical depressive paradox. Just as our personal affairs increasingly seem like the only absolutes we have, they are also made permanently, inchoately under threat from this unseen global totality that trivialises them by comparison. As such, to paraphrase one of Wallace's stories, the defining struggle of the modern psyche has become the management of insignificance: how to reconcile the subjective centrality of our life with its objective meaning-lessness? Whenever it becomes hard to tell 'a good story' about the place we occupy in the world, our sense of ourselves is undermined. And given that so much of the modern world seems unimaginably sophisticated, beyond us on a macro-level, but also just in many everyday respects (Slavoj Žižek's example: who can really picture the inner workings of a computer?), it's not difficult to feel a want of support. Again, only a brief scan of the daily news is needed to realise just *how much* data there is out there, the vast areas of knowledge of which you have only the faintest inkling; the sum total of which nobody is remotely qualified for, and never could be. It may be that the great shared sensation of the information-age is simple incomprehension, bafflement.

One fascinating thing about Houellebecq's books is that they don't seem to be blind to their own contradictions, but are in fact *aware* in a tangled-up sort of way. Their 'realism' entails the thought that novels (and, by extension, stories) are inadequate and delusory, but obviously this is an impossible idea for any novel to hold consistently, and self-hatred is what emerges from the deadlock. It's as though Houellebecq's books were trapped inside narrative. Stuck doing something they know is wrong, but inescapably wrong, the wrongness of which cannot even be expressed properly because there's no way out of story-telling. Something similar is true with respect to identity under globali-sation. It's impossible for me to abandon the stories that give my life shape – that is 'who I am' – but it's also impossible to completely escape the awareness that these stories are flimsy and simplistic and nugatory in relationship to the real, overwhelming complexity and scope of the world. Nietzsche made the point that psychic health demands a minimum of thoughtlessness (what he called 'oblivion'). Too much thinking is bad for you, in other words.[8] So maybe the way to put it is that there are things that can inspire altogether too much consciousness, and globalisation is one of them.

Modernism, as an aesthetic style, was born from the feeling that the old ways of telling stories and making sense of the world had become insufficient. Kurt Vonnegut phrased it perfectly in *Slaughterhouse 5* (1969) when one of his characters says that 'everything there was to know about life' could be found in Dostoyevsky's *The Brothers Karamazov*. 'But that isn't *enough* anymore.' What is there to add? The modernist's project was haunted, and driven, by the idea that it was possible to construct some authentic response to the new circumstances, a better way of living and thinking. Postmodernism could be interpreted as the dismissal of this possibility. There is no authenticity, only various preferences. But here the spectre of depression returns, with its excess of self-consciousness and deficit of self-worth – because if art is nothing more than the gratification of preferences, it's also 'merely' the gratification of preferences. The artistic disorientation discussed in Chapter 2 is a malaise generated by the (real or perceived) absence of external criteria for measuring, or even just expressing, the value of art. And part of what it confronts is the limits of using individual pleasure as a justification of value. The problem is that if art *serves* nothing beyond an individual's pleasure it is also nothing better or more important than self-indulgence – a self that is, in the objective scheme of things, utterly insignificant. It isn't a bad way of outlining what it is that's so naggingly, fuzzily dissatisfying about so much culture at present. This sensation that, however skilfully made a novel or a song or whatever it may be, it's still – in some imprecise way – trivial, peripheral, evanescent, a matter of opinion, or what have you. Joan Didion called the lack of self-respect a condition of being 'locked within oneself... paradoxically incapable of either love or indifference', and I think it's a good description of the type of fidgety anxiety that infects contemporary aesthetics. The cloudy feeling that artistry *ought* to be important, *is* important somehow, but the how and why is unclear.

# 5

# Utopia

The neo-human paradise Houellebecq imagines at the end of *Atomised* returns, ruined, in *The Possibility of an Island*. Where the decoding and reconstruction of the genome meant a cure for the human condition in the former novel, in the latter neo-humans live in a state of numbed isolation, free of death, protected from physical harm, but half-alive, hypnotised with nostalgia for their ancestors' desires. Genetic engineering has not gifted a new identity so much as a hollow copy of an identity, an emptiness undisguised by pain and striving.

*The Possibility of an Island* is told from two points of view. Chapters alternate between Daniel, the human comedian, and his neo-human descendent, Daniel24 – a partially-modified clone of the original Daniel, living by himself in a gated compound roughly two millennia in the future when Earth has been devastated by drought and nuclear war. It emerges that Daniel (or Daniel1, as he is identified) was a witness to the global triumph of the Elohimite Church, a cult – copied by Houellebecq from the real-life Raelian sect – that claims victory over death via the artificial preservation and duplication of human genetic code. Whenever an Elohimite dies, a clone is immediately made as a replacement. Daniel1 was among the first to participate in this procedure, and before committing suicide he records his life story as a testimony to the neo-human dawn. The comedian's insoluble misanthropy, and in particular the relationship with Esther that shattered his will to live, made him, in the eyes of the cult's leaders, 'quite representative of the limitations and contradictions that were to drive the [human] species to ruin'. His autobiography is kept as a monument to the virtues of neo-human modification. In addition to reincarnation, neo-humans have been scripted so as to minimise the power of personal initiative – restlessness being symptomatic of dissatisfaction with one's status as an individual, and therefore the root of will, attachment and desire; the instruments of misery. To this end, a complete repertoire of behaviour was assembled by the neo-human engineers. Psychology is supposed to have become 'as predictable as the functioning of a refrigerator'. The neo-human mind is designed for ascetic contemplation. Infrastructure in the post-apocalyptic world is barely described, though it seems as if it consists of little more an automated Central City, administrating material needs. A quasi-religious ethos exists, but no general society. Individuals live apart and have little more than fleeting, electronic contact with others of their kind. Study of their human origins is encouraged as a touchstone for meditation. The chapters narrated by Daniel24 (succeeded by Daniel25 halfway through the story) take the form of a commentary on Daniel1's life. 'Consciousness of a total determinism was without doubt what differentiated us most clearly from our human predecessors', Daniel25 tells us. However, the neo-human project ends as a failure: both Daniel24 and Daniel25 are corrupted by Daniel1's story, and finally Daniel25 deviates from the behavioural map, leaving his enclosure on a pilgrimage to the site of the first Elohimite Church on Lanzarote. His trip is the novel's 40-page epilogue.

In one obvious sense, Houellebecq's dystopia is just a recent example in a series going back, at least, to Aldous Huxley's *Brave New World* (1932) – a book that's prominently discussed in *Atomised* – of science fiction pitting desensitised, engineered happiness against 'natural', vigorous misery. *The Possibility of an Island*, however, is more like a mirror-image of the iconic scene in *Brave New World*, where the Savage claims the value of poetry, danger, freedom, goodness and sin against medicated peace:

'In fact,' said Mustapha Mond, 'you're claiming the right to be unhappy.'

'All right then,' said the Savage defiantly, 'I'm claiming the right to be unhappy.'

'Not to mention the right to grow old and ugly and impotent; the right to have syphilis and cancer; the right to have too little to eat; the right to be lousy; the right to live in constant apprehension of what may happen tomorrow; the right to catch typhoid; the right to be tortured by unspeakable pains of every kind.' There was a long silence.

'I claim them all,' said the Savage at last.

Mustapha Mond shrugged his shoulders. 'You're welcome,' he said.

In *Possibility* human wants are semi-mythic states for creatures meant to have developed past them. It bears a comparison to that seminal document of human imperfection, Freud's *Civilisation and its Discontents* (1930), and a novel that reads like a dramatic interrogation of that text, Margaret Atwood's *Oryx and Crake* (2003). In *Oryx and Crake*, like *Atomised* and *The Possibility of an Island*, disgust for the human condition motivates the search for a solution through genetic engineering. The disgust belongs to Crake, the God-like scientist who splices together a new type of human animal, and arranges a flood – a laboratory-spawned plague – to sweep away the one already existing. Evaluating his creations, named 'Crake's Children' or 'Crakers':

It was amazing – said Crake – what once-unimaginable things had been accomplished by the team here. What had been altered was nothing less than the ancient primate brain. Gone were its destructive features, the features responsible for the world's current illnesses. For instance, racism... had been eliminated in the model group, merely by switching the bonding mechanism: the [Crakers] simply did not register skin colour. Hierarchy could not exist among them, because they lacked the neural complexes that would have created it. …the king-of-the-castle hard-wiring that had plagued humanity had, in them, been unwired. They ate nothing but leaves and grass and roots and a berry or two; thus their foods were plentiful and always available. Their sexuality was not a constant torment to them, not a cloud of turbulent hormones: they came into heat at regular intervals, as did most mammals other than man.

In fact there would never be anything for these people to inherit, there would be no family trees, no marriages, and no divorces. They were perfectly adjusted to their habitat, so they would never have to create houses or tools or weapons, or, for that matter, clothing. They would have no need to invent any harmful symbolisms, such as kingdoms, icons, gods, or money. Best of all, they recycled their own excrement.

The Crakers are designed to expire at thirty. Fear of death, the very foreknowledge of it, is edited out of their brains. So too the want of religion (the 'G-Spot', Crake calls it). The great irony of *Oryx and Crake* is that, after the apocalypse and Crake's death, it takes mythology to lure the Children out from the lab into the world bequeathed to them – the seed for the religion that takes shape at the novel's climax with Crake as its godhead, the creator celebrated against his design. A similar irony is at play in *The Possibility of an Island* where it gradually becomes clear that the neo-humans have their own ideas of paradise; their own belief, in fact, in a race of supreme beings that will succeed them – the mysterious Future Ones, whose perfection is such that they are almost impossible to conceive. 'The Future Ones, unlike us, will not be machines, nor truly separate beings. They will be one, whilst also being many. Nothing can give us an exact image of the nature of the Future Ones.' The gods have their own gods.

The infamous conceit of *Civilisation and its Discontents* is that it is not merely the particular civilisation or society we happen to inhabit that generates human neuroses, it is civilisation *as such* that does this, since it is impossible to reconcile the restrictions needed to keep a social group together with the satisfaction of individual desires. More substantially, the irreconcilability between the urge to belong in society and the urge to meet one's own appetites is a non-contingent part of human nature. Untranquil, frustrated animals is *what we are*; fundamentally mal-adapted and misshapen. Psychoanalysis might be seen as offering a retort, of a fashion, to the religious-mystic idea that the path to fulfilment is through the elimination of desire and the exultation of immediate being – even if such a state were achievable, it would be (in the proper sense of the word) inhuman. The engineered beings in *The Possibility of an Island* are creatures in which the dilemma has been attacked but not defeated. Harmful natural impulses have been deprogrammed, but the mental spaces these impulses occupied are left unfilled, leaving the neo-humans with the sensation that they have been diluted rather than enhanced. 'Planning the extinction of desire in Buddhist-like terms,' says Daniel25, '[the Elohimite designers] had banked on the maintenance of a weakened, non-tragic energy, purely conservative in nature, which would have continued to enable the functioning of thought... This phenomenon had only been produced in insignificant proportions, and it was, on the contrary, sadness, melancholy, languid and finally mortal apathy that had submerged our disincarnated generations. The most patent indicator of failure was that I had ended up envying the destiny of Daniel1.' If human nature were truly corrected, it is possible we would be unable to sympathise with, or even relate to, its products (which is why the Future Ones are, necessarily, unimaginable). In the end it is the anomaly, the 'weakness', of religion that makes the Crakers intriguing.

Unfortunately, up until the epilogue, the dystopian scenes in *The Possibility of an Island* rather confirm the dullness of neo-human life by being solemn, obscure and laughably unconvincing bits of fiction (Daniel24, a posthuman monk, still insists on calling his penis his 'virile member', for whatever reason). *Possibility* is disagreeable on purpose – Houellebecq has some fun (insofar as Daniel, the celebrity shock-comic, resembles Michel Houellebecq, the provocateur author) implying that his audience are stupid to listen to him, and that he hates them – but it's a rotten piece of work largely because there's so much mud between the scenes where its real interests lie. Transparently, the energy core in the book is not genetic engineering, or posthumanity, or cults, or the state of Western civilisation, but mortal frenzy. The bitterness about human embodiment that simmered through *Whatever* and *Atomised* boils up, at the end of Daniel1's story, into a kind of ecstasy of hatred:

it wasn't long before the heat settled on the south of Spain; naked young girls began to tan themselves, especially on weekends, on the beach near the residence, and I began to feel the return, albeit weak and flaccid, of something that wasn't even really desire – for the word would seem to me, despite everything, to imply a minimum belief in the possibility of its fulfilment – but the memory, the phantom of what could have been desire. I could now make out clearly the *cosa mentale* [the desire for desire], the ultimate torment, and at that moment I could say at last that I understood. Sexual pleasure was not only superior, in refinement and violence, to all other pleasures life had to offer; it was not only the one pleasure with which there was no collateral damage to the organism, but which on the contrary contributes to maintaining it at its highest level of vitality and strength; it was in truth the sole pleasure, the sole objective of human existence, and all other pleasures – whether associated with rich food, tobacco, alcohol or drugs – were only derisory and desperate compensations, mini-suicides that did not have the courage to speak their name, attempts to speed up the destruction of a body that no longer had access to the one real pleasure. Thus human life was organised in a terribly simple fashion, and for twenty years or so, in my scripts and sketches, I had pussy-footed around a reality that I could have expressed in just a few sentences. Youth was the time for happiness, its only season; young people, leading a lazy, carefree life, partially occupied by scarcely absorbing studies, were able to devote themselves unlimitedly to the liberated exultation of their bodies. They could play, dance, love and multiply their pleasures. They could leave a party, in the early hours of the morning, in the company of sexual partners they had chosen, and contemplate the dreary line of employees going to work. … Later on, having started a family, having entered the adult world, they would be introduced to worry, work, responsibility and the difficulties of existence; they would have to pay taxes, submit themselves to administrative formalities whilst ceaselessly bearing witness – powerless and shamefilled – to the irreversible degradation of their own bodies... From this sad life, marked by shame, all joy would be pitilessly banished. When they wanted to draw near to young people's bodies, they would be chased away, rejected, ridiculed, insulted and, more and more often nowadays, imprisoned. The physical bodies of young people, the only desirable possession the world has ever produced, were reserved for the exclusive use of the young, and the fate of the old was to work and to suffer. This was the true meaning of *solidarity between generations*; it was a pure and simple holocaust of each generation in favour of the one that replaced it, a cruel, prolonged holocaust that brought with it no consolation, no comfort, nor any material or emotional compensation.

This is probably the most unvarnished passage in Houellebecq's fiction. That it is hysterical, reductive, ugly, inconsistent (since earlier in the book Daniel says it's not sex that is most desirable, but sex with love), and involves more than one false generalisation is also quite true. But it has a pulse the rest of the book, for the most part, lacks. Still – to digress for a moment – it's tempting to say that the failure of *The Possibility of an Island* is not only that there's too much padding between the bits where its blood rises, but also that there's not enough when it finally does. In *Atomised* it's Bruno who acts as Houellebecq's avatar for his theories about sex and its resemblance to free-market capitalism, but there the disenchantment is at least tempered by humour and pity, e.g. during his farcical visit to the Lieu de Changement, or the variously inept efforts at seduction ('I had to stick to my "liberal humanist" position', he notes, bitterly, 'I knew in my heart that it was my only chance of getting laid'), or the brilliantly banal awfulness of the scenes describing his and Christiane's visits to Parisian sex clubs, where Bruno 'could not help but feel that many of the women they met... were somewhat disappointed when they saw his penis. No one ever commented; their courtesy was exemplary, and the atmosphere was always friendly and polite; but their looks couldn't lie and slowly he realised that, from a sexual viewpoint, he just didn't make the grade.' Whereas *The Possibility of an Island* is almost totally humourless, starring a comedian who hates laughter ('you always end up crashing into the same difficulty, which is that life, fundamentally, *is not* comical'), and whose egotism is barely embellished. The novel is an archetypal work of post-fame indulgence, simultaneously 'purer' and less appealing. It can be a minor shock, actually, to return to *Atomised* after *Possibility* and to realise how conventionally tender much of the earlier book is – in the passages recalling the young Djerzinski's life with his grandmother, for instance; or the death of his lover. In *Possibility*, on the other hand, everything is fully subsumed to the numbers and figures of erotic pleasure – how much you can get, with who, for how long; the unequal resources and their bullying power; the hierarchies and basic indifference of the haves for the have-nots. For Daniel and the other Houellebecq hedonists, what's suffered is not some philosophical or artistic disorientation, but a super-orientation, a *surplus*-orientation: they know too well what they want. It's this clarity that disorientates art and philosophy, by making everything so blindingly simple. But the more plainly Houellebecq insists the more specious he seems. This is the peculiarity of truth in art – that truth should require 'art' (a synonym for deception, as we know) to make itself felt. It's why *The Possibility of an Island*, although it contains the least 'pussyfooting' of all the books, lacks purchase.

The science-fiction in *Atomised* and *The Possibility of an Island* is interesting mainly for its poverty. Neither case is well-imagined, nor do they play a key role in the stories they belong to. Unlike the grandiose philosophising or lurid sex writing, it's pretty easy to imagine both novels functioning just as well without the futurism. *Atomised* could have stopped at the results of Djerzinski's research, not least because the nirvana it creates is barely sketched before the book finishes. Almost all the (neo-human) narrator tells us is that:

> Having broken the filial chain that linked us to humanity, we live on. Men consider us to be happy; it is certainly true that we have succeeded in overcoming the monstrous egotism, cruelty and anger which they could not; we live very different lives. Science and art are still part of our society, but without the stimulus of personal vanity, the pursuit of Truth and Beauty has taken on a less urgent aspect. To humans of the old species, our world seems a paradise.

*Possibility*'s dystopia, although it's described in much greater detail, may exist only to debunk the promise made in *Atomised*. The key difference between the two futures is that in *Atomised* sex has been done away with; whereas in the later book, although the neo-humans do not have sex, their 'sexual biochem-istry... had remained almost identical' with that of humans. This 'was undoubtedly the real reason for the sensation of suffocation and malaise', reports Daniel25, 'that overcame me as I advanced through Daniel1's story'. So it is still sex, indirectly, that disrupts the neo-humans and causes their unhappiness, Houellebecq seeming literally (and literarily) incapable of imagining life otherwise. His utopias are either empty or they crumble under the old pressures of human life. Marcuse described the inability to imagine historical difference as the atrophy of the utopian imagination, and it seems supremely fitting that Houellebecq's fiction – perhaps *the* literary product from the underbelly of the liberal-capitalist End of History – so thoroughly fails to envision a better world.

But the genetic manipulation in Houellebecq's novels is also another way the books have of expressing their self-contempt. Literature is sometimes called the 'spooky art'. I think usually what this is meant to describe is the writer's feeling that she is not in control of what she writes about; how a story 'chooses them', as they say, rather than the other way round – inspiration is always something of an enigma. But a spooky element is part of reading too. The poststructuralist idea that text doesn't require an author to be meaningful (that the author 'dies' once they've laid their words on paper) is true insomuch as it means that the meaning of a piece of writing isn't fixed, but lives variously through its readers. Since the personal associations and pleasure-centres that colour stories from reader to reader are so often subconscious or half-realised, the effect of a powerful piece of fiction is rarely felt rationally, but as something more immediate, sensational – 'spooky'. There's an old Platonic idea that truth is already known in the soul, only we constantly need to be reminded of it. When literature hits the nerves powerfully it's not unlike this: a shock of recognition. The thought (cf. Hemmingway) that it does no good to talk about some parts of writing transmits the fact that, after a certain point, to talk about writing in general is to leave out the singular effect it has on the reader; the sense in which a story is theirs alone. Whenever the objection is made that theorising about literature somehow misses the point, that it intellectualises needlessly and spoils pleasure in the process, it's right at least that there is a core, incommunicably personal aspect to the reader's experience that gains little or nothing from analysis. It's also a truism that the imagination is not the servant of the intellect, and may frequently be at odds with it, so this is another natural limit to explaining art's charm. Literature as we know it involves a twin-failure of explanation – the writer who can't really explain where writing comes from, the reader who can't really explain what it does.

The threat Heidegger identified in modern science is that it might eliminate the universe's 'dark spots', the gaps in our understanding that give us the space to invent meaning. For example, the scientific explanation of thunder destroys the ignorance that allowed men to project meaning onto the weather (that the thunder was God's anger, e.g.). The radical possibility opened by neuroscience is of demystifying and de-meaning art itself, of throwing light onto the dark spots of inspiration and aesthetic enjoyment. Douglas Coupland's novel *Generation A* (2009) presents one intriguing possibility of genetic engineering: a drug is manufactured that recreates the peace of deep reading. It is, in effect, one of the benefits of literature in pill form. Science-fiction interested in brain science is always, consciously or not, thinking about itself, exploring the possibility of writing's obsolescence – of a time when inner feeling and moral education are matters for technical expertise rather than personal judgment. *Oryx and Crake* is a parable in precisely this vein. The narrator, Jimmy, Crake's best friend and the Last Man-figure left with the Crakers after the apocalypse, engages in fruitless debates with Crake over the value of art. He is doubly-limited, understanding neither the scientist's genetic breakthroughs, nor the motivations of Oryx, Crake's inscrutable lover, with whom Jimmy has an affair. The novel can be read as an old-fashioned morality tale about the cost of playing God, where, upon discovering Jimmy's tryst with Oryx, Crake is driven mad and destroyed by all-too-human jealousy. But it is unclear, in the end, where the real explanation for Crake's actions lies. Partly, the ambiguity seeps in because his 'fall' is the spur for the terrible act of destruction (unleashing the plague) rather than a consequence of his folly. Atwood leaves it elegantly undecided how much Crake knew and how far ahead he planned; whether Jimmy was his antagonist or puppet, or both. The everyman narrator is left with two brute facts – his obsessive love for Oryx, and the catastrophe that followed. But why they happened, how each connects to the other, is unknown. There is no story. The denouncement comes with the climactic discovery, by 'Snowman' (Jimmy's post-apocalyptic guise), of a letter in the ruins of Crake's laboratory, written by Jimmy in the aftermath of the plague:

> He picks [the letter] up with curiosity. What is it that the Jimmy he'd once been had seen fit to communicate, or at least to record – to set down in black and white, with smudges – for the edification of a world that no longer existed?
>
> 'To whom it may concern... Crake himself had developed a vaccine concurrently with the virus, but he had destroyed it prior to his ~~assisted suicide~~ death. ... As for Crake's motives, I can only speculate. Perhaps...'
>
> Here the handwriting stops. Whatever Jimmy's speculations might have been on the subject of Crake's motives, they had not been recorded. Snowman crumples the sheets up, drops them onto the floor. It's the fate of these words to be eaten by beetles.

As in Houellebecq, the territory between the simplicity of biological urge and the immaculate principles of science is dark, and not necessarily meaningful. There is a metaphysical question about the truth of human experience beneath the double-effect materialism has on self-perception. Again, although in one way materialism makes (or appears to make) life flatter and more easily explicable – by revealing general principles for behaviour in terms of biology, psychology, etc.; by dispelling religious superstition – in another it is deeply confusing, because there is a sense in which ignorance and delusion are fundamental parts of human identity, and yet materialism seems to allow no space for this. At one moment in *The Possibility of an Island* Daniel25 mentions the theory that consciousness is a 'software fiction', a hopelessly misleading picture of the world, unable even to comprehend its own workings. Neuroscience demonstrates nothing so much as the distance between the unimaginably complex flesh and blood mechanisms of the brain and our naïve, conscious self-image. Only an inferential awareness of the vast data-banks and reservoirs of knowledge about human workings is enough to compel a besieged kind of thought that you must not know yourself very well. Stanislaw Lem's beautiful description of incomprehension at the phenomena on an immense, alien planet in *Solaris* (1961) is highly appropriate: 'We know, but cannot grasp, that above and below, beyond the limits of perception or imagination, thousands of millions of simultaneous transformations are at work, interlinked like a musical score by mathematical counterpoint', a 'symphony... but we lack the ears to hear it.' Not an alien planet, our material reality is the thing we know but cannot grasp, and it is human science that tells us what we cannot imagine, insofar as we are unable to accept the message. Rather than simply dispel our illusions, at some root level materialism seems to only inform us that we have illusions, but leaves them in place. Subjectivity is left stranded; a bewildered, stupid thing, untuned to itself or the world. Both depressive realism and fiction imagining the possibilities of brain science confront a type of event-horizon for literature, in aiming for a truth no longer grounded in meaning – the dumb, physical process behind the activity of story-telling.

***

The epilogue of *The Possibility of an Island* tracks Daniel25 walking from his dwelling in San Jose, Spain, through the ruins of Madrid, and then toward Lanzarote over the dried sea. Unlike earlier chapters from the dystopia, the narrative attains some shape and a peaceful rhythm as the neo-human travels across the desolate landscape, away from the protection of his compound and the mechanisms that guarantee his resurrection. He is accompanied by his dog Fox, a clone of Daniel1's corgi (and all-purpose literary symbol of innocent *joie de vivre*). The journey bears a resemblance to the last chapter of *Whatever*, after the anonymous narrator has left the psychiatric hospital – his bile eased into a tranquilised sadness: 'it's been a while since meaning of my actions has seemed clear to me;' he says, 'they don't seem clear very often, let's say. The rest of the time I'm more or less *in the position of the observer.*' On impulse, the narrator of *Whatever* books a trip to the countryside, renting a bike and cycling through deserted forests, breaking into sobs from time to time for no clear reason. Unique among Houellebecq's protagonists, he has been diagnosed with depression, and so his realism is officially sick. 'The formula seems a happy one to me. It's not that I feel tremendously low; it's rather that the world around me appears high.' The story concludes with self-imprisonment, a barren end to desire:

> For years I have been walking alongside a phantom who looks like me, and who lives in a theoretical paradise strictly related to the world. I've long believed it was up to me to become one

with this phantom. That's done with.

I cycle still further into the forest. ... The landscape is more and more gentle, amiable, joyous; my skin hurts. I am at the heart of the abyss. I feel my skin again as a frontier, and the external world as a crushing weight. The impression of separation is total...

In *The Possibility of an Island*, Daniel25 and Fox's final adventure aptly summarises Houellebecq's sensibility, albeit not enticingly. Grandiose metaphysical reflections mix with armchair sociology ('Nothing now remains of those literary and artistic productions of which mankind had been so proud... we could no longer see in it anything more than the arbitrary ravings of limited and confused minds'), garish sentimentality bangs up against grave pronunciations about the brutality of existence. There is even a half-hearted swipe at his original target, the post-Sixties sexual marketplace. A small number of humans have survived the end of the world, although they have regressed into a state of savagery ('slightly more intelligent monkeys, and, for this reason, more dangerous'). Daniel25 happens across a large tribe and wastes no time with his judgments. He notes copulation with females is reserved for the dominant males, with all other men pitilessly rejected. 'In short, it was a mode of organisation that quite closely recalled that of human societies, in particular those of the last periods... a social system of control of access to the vulva of the females, in order to maintain the genetic makeup of the species.' (Later adding, a trifle self-consciously: 'they were only the caricature-like residues of the worst tendencies of ordinary mankind'.) The savages fight among themselves, ritually slaughter their elderly, and kill Fox while Daniel25 is distracted.[9] In his review of *Platform*, Julian Barnes drew a hopeful analogy between Houellebecq and Camus, 'who began by creating in Meursault one of the most disaffected characters in postwar fiction, ended by writing "The First Man," in which ordinary lives are depicted with the richest observation and sympathy. The trajectory of Houellebecq's world view will be worth following.' In the event, rather than turn his sympathy outwards, Houellebecq intensified his bitterness and solipsism to a hideous degree. It gives *Possibility* its most oppressively effective passages, but by the time we arrive at the exhausted symbolism of the epilogue it's hard to think how it could be taken further. In that respect, the comparatively long wait between *Possibility* and *La Carte et le Territoire* isn't surprising. Houellebecq's imagined world ends up as flat and sterile as the neo-humans who live there, a zone where everything is settled, and so nothing lives – life has been crushed out of it. 'The animal world was known, human societies were known; no mystery was hidden in it, and nothing could be expected from it, except the repetition of carnage.'

Although not apocalyptic, *La Carte et le Territoire* is also fixated with a subject of depleted energy, and resigned to social rot. It spans ninety years and ends deep in the twenty-first century. Tracing the life of Jed Martin, a famous photographer and painter, the novel provides an image of a France in decay. Here too, the world of the future has atrophied instead of evolved, petrifying in the grip of capitalism. Money pervades everything. Jed becomes fabulously wealthy painting portraits of leading businessmen, his stratospheric prices dictated by the mechanism of supply and demand rather than any inherent quality of the work. Jed's father – an architect who dreamed of being an artist – is incrementally killed by capital. As a young man, his projects won't sell, and financial necessity soon forces him to abandon his visions for a job in an architectural firm. 'Life immediately became less amusing', he recalls to his son. Dying of colon cancer, the old man finally travels to Dignitas to purchase an assisted suicide; even his death is marked with a price. The names of social reformers appear throughout *La Carte et le Territoire*: Jed's father was a member of an art collective who idolised William

Morris; the character 'Michel Houellebecq' collects books by Karl Marx and Charles Fourier. But this seems only to underline the utter failure of utopian hopes. Social protectionism in France steadily disappears; its entitlement culture ends, and the market is unfettered. Ultimately the country itself becomes a product, a simulacrum of its historical self, peddling the 'fantasy image' of France to armies of tourists from Asia and the Americas.

In *The Possibility of an Island*, the religious-mystic idea is the only alternative Houellebecq seems able to present against this animal pain and striving. If nothing is good, the good must be nothing. Curiously, it's Daniel1, rather than any of his neo-human successors, who gives the clearest articulation to this, during a dreamlike experience inside a Elohimite artwork: 'I was... seized by an intense desire to disappear, to melt into a luminous, active nothingness, vibrating with perpetual possibilities; the luminosity became blinding, the space around me seemed to explode and diffract into shards of light, but it was not a space in the usual sense of the term, it included many dimensions, and any other form of perception had disappeared – this space contained, in the conventional sense of the word, nothing.' Appropriately, the finest moments in *Possibility*'s epilogue are the most unearthly. Daniel25 gives up the idea of finding the First Church on Lanzarote, but continues numbly onwards through the nuclear desert to the sea. 'Under my feet the ashes became white, and the sky took on ultramarine tones... It was three days later, in the early hours, that I saw the clouds. Their silky surface appeared to be just a modulation on the horizon, a trembling of light, and I first thought of a mirage, but on closer approach I made out more clearly cumulus clouds of beautiful matt white, separated by supernaturally still, thin curls of vapour.' The novel loses itself in clouds, ending with Daniel25 cocooned a living death; nullified but still existing – a mere gesture of disembodied blankness, impure anti-matter.

## 6

# There is Actually
# No Such Thing as Atheism

Claiming that Houellebecq is an especially resonant author is not to say that he's utterly and unquestionably convincing. In some obvious ways, he misrepresents life. The novels make close to no mention of friendship, or community, or the pleasures of achievement, and the toxic attitude towards parenting has been mentioned already. Houellebecq spins his cynicism out into an all-consuming theory, and has no patience for anything that fails to fit this theory – 'like a sick man who wants the entire world to suffer', as Voltaire said of Pascal. It's not hard to disagree with life as Houellebecq depicts it; at least it's not hard to say that he's excluding an awful lot. But then there's a difference between reasoned truths and truth-*effects*: the almost percussive feeling of invigoration or quickening or clear-sight that comes with certain powerful aesthetic experiences. What people mean when they say they were 'struck' by art. To my mind, the force and counter-intuitive vitality of Houellebecq's writing is rather comforting evidence of literature's continuing ability to resonate in hostile circumstances – which is just to say that, at its best, his work manages to *feel true* in a way that's rare. As I've tried to demonstrate, the merit of this (bleak, miserable, contempt-filled) feeling of truth becomes very quickly complicated and murky once you start thinking about it, and it drives us towards large and stupefying questions about why we want truth in art, or how we know it when we find it, or if it even exists. But for me the initial, percussive sensation is undeniable. It feels as though it's owed an explanation.

Whenever pessimism is elevated into a philosophical system,

as though to prove that misery is the truth of human existence, it meets a kind of natural incredulity. Why should we believe that we are unhappy all the time? Or be horrified at our own existence? Disappointment and sadness are parts of life – one might respond – but so is happiness (that's only common sense), and the pessimist omits or denies pleasures whose reality is self-evident to any normal person. Whilst admitting this, and admitting that it's perverse to glorify misery for its own sake, at the core of depressive realism is something much harder to deflect, and all of the inconsistencies, shrillness and tendencies toward self-romance involved in pessimistic art don't rid us of the trouble. Houellebecq dramatises one great, largely unspoken yet almost tactile anxiety running through Western culture – the anxiety that can be grasped by simply thinking long enough about any normal advertisement and the visions of the better, happier, more self-possessed you it tries to conjure. Health and pleasure and comfort cannot last. *You will die.* This is not one defeat amidst life's pleasures; it is the overwhelming end, a negation at once absolute and utterly private. The comparison between Houellebecq and Pascal is fitting. 'Let us imagine a number of people in chains,' Pascal wrote in the *Pensees*, 'all of them sentenced to death, some of them slaughtered every day before the eyes of the others, the remaining ones seeing their own fate in that of their neighbours, looking at each other in pain and despair, waiting their turn. This is the image of the human condition.' Death is the terrifying, singular fact consciousness tries to suppress, although it can never do this completely. But for Pascal waking someone up to the truth of their mortality was a profound mission – if you compel a person to face the misery of death, you force them to look for a remedy, i.e. to embark on the (difficult) path of virtuous Christian life. The truth is hard but it is also liberating, because it enables us to see the unhappiness and self-deception that drives most of our activity, and the extent to which we fill our minds simply to avoid thinking about our death-marked condition. Diversion, says Pascal, 'is the only comfort we have in our misery, and yet it is the greatest of our miseries; for... it brings us imperceptibly to our death'. Much like a later Christian philosopher, Simone Weil, Pascal enjoys the dubious quality of giving a stark and uncomfortably astute portrait of existential woe, for which the only cure is faith – but a faith that's inimical to the modern, materialist world. Needless to say, there is no supernatural remedy in Houellebecq's novels (nor, if *The Possibility of an Island* is taken as the last word, even a scientific one), and so the consequence appears to be that knowing the truth is no use, and if we cannot ignore it entirely we should at least pursue the diversions that allow us to forget about it as much as possible (sex, in Houellebecq's opinion). Houellebecq is hardly the first person to articulate this thought, but he might have given it its boldest modern setting. The miserable truth remains, without salvation, which brings us back to what was almost the first question asked in this book. What good is a truth like that?

Alain Badiou has said that the most straightforward definition of religion is as a means for maintaining the link between truth and meaning. 'God moves in mysterious ways' amounts to the thought that, although we may not know how all the (potentially terrible) things that happen to us fit into a plan, we can rest assured that they *do* fit a plan, somehow. Materialism denies any such guarantee. In Houellebecq's novels death and decline are unavoidable facts of existence, but they don't really *signify* anything. They are senseless truths, corresponding to no intention or design. As you will have gathered, the paradoxical (or, if you like, hypocritical) aspects of Houellebecq's fiction are generally a direct result of his materialist philosophy, since materialism breeds distrust for stories. One good example of this, taken from political theory, is the classic materialist critique of ideology – *viz* that in order to disguise or placate material inequalities certain social fictions are invented, which restore equality on an imaginary plane. In the Marxist version of this argument, economic injustice is soothed because in other, 'more important' respects everybody is convinced that they as well-off as everybody else, e.g. equal before God, or as citizens of the State. Without the underlying material imbalance, however, there would be no need for these equalising myths. When Marx described religion as 'the opium of the people' he meant it in the sense of a painkiller rather than a source of pleasure. Not something wicked *per se*; a relief (of sorts) from discomfort – but ultimately a solace that prolongs the very suffering it eases, because it obscures the true causes of pain. Even if you don't think this is an exhaustive explanation of how religion comes to be, the coping mechanism it identifies is powerful and real. Needless to say, the fictions that disguise inequality don't present themselves as fictions, which would defeat the point. So a present-day equivalent – now that people are typically less religious and more politically disengaged – would be like the idea that anyone can be happy if only they have the right attitude, or successful if they work hard enough; in general, the kind of propositions which make subjective well-being a matter of individual responsibility, rather than something largely at the mercy of impersonal forces. One of the great pains of materialism, which is no less painful even if it can sound a little trite, is that it turns us into objects – fixed and limited things – and thereby exposes all the mental-contortions we go through to cover up the fact that we aren't the smartest, or strongest, or youngest, or most beautiful, or successful, or admired person there is; on top of which we are ceaselessly and helplessly growing older, and will one day die. It wouldn't be much of an exaggeration to say that Houellebecq's founding act as a writer was the application of this kind of materialist critique to romance, so that romantic or erotic happiness are deemed to have nothing essentially mysterious about them, but depend only on objectively identifiable criteria about someone's body and circumstances. Having the right attitude (the right brain) is sheer luck, an accident of birth like everything else.

But there's a limit to the idea that you can strip away all the consoling lies people tell themselves to find the real material truth underneath, and to his credit Houellebecq is aware of it. During one scene in *Whatever*, the luckless Tisserand confides his reasons for not visiting prostitutes: 'Maybe I'll end up doing it', he says. 'But I know that some men can get the same thing for free, *and with love to boot*. I prefer trying; for the moment I still prefer trying.' The status of this remark is ambiguous. On the one hand, it is made clear that Tisserand is not in control of the forces at work: he is physically repulsive and not much of a personality either. His longing is wildly out of line with anything he can realistically expect. But, on the other, it is also clear that renouncing his desire would be devastating for him, and – as the narrator of *Whatever* acknowledges – the refusal to give up on love is basically admirable. It gives Tisserand hope, however much it hurts.

The nobility of Tisserand's resolve reminds us of a more fundamental truth besides: we all need our stories. As Slavoj Žižek remarks, in an essay about the election of President Obama, cynicism is its own type of foolishness in this regard:

The position of the cynic is that he alone holds some piece of terrible, unvarnished wisdom. The paradigmatic cynic tells you privately, in a confidential low-key voice: 'But don't you get it that it is all really about (money/power/sex), that all high principles and values are just empty phrases which count for nothing?' What the cynics don't see is their own naivety, the naivety of their cynical wisdom that ignores the power of illusions.

Undoubtedly we all employ ego-preserving fictions in order to compensate for our limitations and inequalities. Does it follow that these are *nothing more* than fictions? Žižek's answer is an emphatic 'No'. Pure cynicism is inconsistent and impossible because it suggests that you could step outside narrative and find reality. But reality is partially structured by the stories we tell ourselves. There is a sense in which, for instance, the ideal of justice is a 'lie', given that in practice the law habitually favours the privileged and discriminates against the powerless. But, Žižek argues, this fiction also creates the real possibility of emancipation, because it allows the disenfranchised to confront the powers that be with their hypocrisy. The lie can transform reality. Likewise, Tisserand's irrational belief in love is the only way he stands a chance of finding it. So it ends up being perversely rational after all. For him, 'realism' would be a tomb. This is why, although Tisserand dies before he finds any solace, the narrator of *Whatever* is not wrong to salute his memory: 'At least, I said to myself on learning of his death, he'll have battled to the end... in his heart there was still the struggle, the desire and the will to struggle.'

It's a truism of self-help that a person's quality of life is (at least partially) determined by their self-image; that is, the stories they tell about themselves. If someone can be made to perceive their character in a new light, then it allows them to behave differently – reality changes. In a commencement speech he gave at Kenyon College in 2005, David Foster Wallace also stressed the idea that controlling perspective is something intrinsic to self-respect, although as he conceived it self-respect has more to do with forgetting, rather than asserting, yourself:

The only thing that's capital-T True is that you get to decide how you're going to try to see it. You get to consciously decide what has meaning and what doesn't. You get to decide what to worship.

Because here's something else that's true. In the day-to-day trenches of adult life, there is actually no such thing as atheism. There is no such thing as not worshipping. Everybody worships. The only choice we get is what to worship. And an outstanding reason for choosing some sort of God or spiritual-type thing to worship – be it J.C. or Allah, be it Yahweh or the Wiccan mother-goddess or the Four Noble Truths or some infrangible set of ethical principles – is that pretty much anything else you worship will eat you alive. If you worship money and things – if they are where you tap real meaning in life – then you will never have enough. Never feel you have enough. It's the truth. Worship your own body and beauty and sexual allure and you will always feel ugly, and when time and age start showing, you will die a million deaths before they finally plant you. On one level, we all know this stuff already – it's been codified as myths, proverbs, clichés, bromides, epigrams, parables: the skeleton of every great story. The trick is keeping the truth up-front in daily consciousness. Worship power – you will feel weak and afraid, and you will need ever more power over others to keep the fear at bay. Worship your intellect, being seen as smart – you will end up feeling stupid, a fraud, always on the verge of being found out. And so on.

On the face of it, this might seem like no more than a smooth argument for something insipid,[10] e.g. the kind of power-within-you positive thinking Barbara Ehrenreich tore to shreds in *Smile or Die* (2010), her memoir of breast cancer and the relentlessly upbeat support-networks it brought her into contact with – a 'tyranny of positive thinking' claiming the power of life-or-death. As Ehrenreich recalls:

there was, I learned, an urgent medical reason to embrace cancer with a smile: a 'positive attitude' is supposedly essential to recovery. During the months when I was under-going chemotherapy, I encountered this assertion over and over – on websites, in books, from oncology nurses and fellow sufferers. Eight years later, it remains almost axiomatic, within the breast cancer culture, that survival hinges on 'attitude'. One study found 60% of women who had been treated for the disease attributing their continued survival to a 'positive attitude'.

Contrary to this, the research Ehrenreich examined indicated not only that subjective feelings make no difference to patients' chances of survival, but 'one 2004 study even found, in complete contradiction to the tenets of positive thinking, that women who perceive more benefits from their cancer "tend to face a poorer quality of life – including worse mental functioning – compared with women who do not perceive benefits from their diagnoses."' Putting a winsome face on cancer is punishing work. As much as anything, it demands the repression of entirely justified feelings of anger and fear. 'This is a great convenience for health workers and even friends of the afflicted, who might prefer fake cheer to complaining,' noted Ehrenreich, 'but it is not so easy on the afflicted.' It would be easy to see Ehrenreich's story as just more evidence, if we needed it, of how ultimately helpless we are over life-determining contingencies, and the speciousness of asserting that 'you get to decide how you're going to try to see it', come what may. But Wallace is saying more than that. His point is not that you can learn to accept anything, if only you believe in the right way. It's that there's no opting-out of belief. *You have to worship something.* The cynic is never a true cynic, because in practice he can't help but follow some idea about what's meaningful, even if he never admits it to himself.

The claim Wallace makes that in 'the day-to-day trenches of adult life, there is actually no such thing as atheism' isn't really an accusation of hypocrisy (i.e. that you're kidding yourself if you don't believe in God), but it does touch upon a genuine shortcoming in contemporary secular thinking. The immediate difficulty in atheism is not that it precludes some comforting illusions, or introduces a catastrophic dose of meaninglessness into our lives (absurd on the face of it – we go on living don't we?), but that we're obliged to face up to the groundlessness of certain beliefs that persist whether we give them a religious expression or not, e.g. the unfathomable quality of 'humanity' as substituted for the unfathomable quality of 'soul'. It's as though the world-weary dismissal of religion – the one saying it would be nice to believe in these comforting fairly tales, but unfortunately it's impossible – could be turned on its head: it would be nice not to believe in absurd, unjustifiable things, but unfortunately we do. I've said that the truth as depressive realism sees it is so grim it's hard to understand why it's worth telling, and in fact depressive realism can't tell us why – it simply assumes that it is. In trying to dispose of all untrustworthy ideals, the pessimist ends up demonstrating how indispensable (some kind of) faith is, even if it's only a faith in your own hard-eyed veracity. Joseph Ratzinger put it well in his *Introduction to Christianity* (1969), and one needn't be religious to take the point:

> Anyone who makes up his mind to evade the uncertainty of belief will have to experience the uncertainty of unbelief, which can never finally eliminate for certain the possibility that belief may after all be the truth. It is not until belief is rejected that its unrejectability becomes evident.

If what Wallace and Ratzinger say is right, the upshot is that we are each effectively in a position of being forced to adopt some belief about what makes life meaningful. But even if we're able to exercise some choice about what this is, there's no way of validating our decision. Belief is never certain. The act of belief – the forced choice – comes before any theoretical justification, which is why in the last analysis belief always appears unaccountable or contingent. According to Kierkegaard, faith and doubt are concurrent: humans are never sure, ultimately we only 'believe that we believe', and are unable to escape the fear of being deluded. This is just to generalise Sontag's remark about justifying art: our beliefs about what matters can never be proven, they can only be made more or less plausible. Houellebecq's fiction is built from the idea that the most plausible thing of all to believe is the materialist hypothesis that we are each born alone, live alone, and die alone – and this is depressing. It trivialises art, because it undermines communion; it sabotages love in the same way. After everything else, you are alone, which is not good. It's no accident that the forms of worship Wallace claimed would 'eat you alive' are all essentially forms of self-worship. Selfishness (irony of ironies) is self-defeating, since it's impossible to sustain. No matter how much you consume, you never have enough; on top of which there's no outrunning ageing or death. So we get the result that what seems truest of all – our deep, immediate self-centredness – is also a hateful curse we would be fortunate to dispel. How? Infuriatingly, the problem of selfishness creates a vicious logical circle: if I make a decision to act less selfishly, isn't it only because, in the end, I think I'll be better off in some way? – i.e. isn't it *still* a selfish decision, and therefore provides no escape from selfishness? This deadlock is why some philosophers, such as Weil, claimed you would need the help of an 'impossible', supernatural force (God's grace) to realise selflessness at all. But it's worth pointing out that, if only in a very small way, the basic uncertainty of belief transforms into something of an asset when we're trying to think outside ourselves. As the joke goes, every man would dearly like to be an egotist, but none of them can quite manage it: even what appears to us as our most powerful and logically compelling motivation – self-interest – is doubtful, and it's impossible to be finally convinced that selfishness *is* what behaviour reduces to, even if we think it would be better to have no altruistic illusions.

\*\*\*

One of the oldest problems in moral philosophy is how to articulate the idea that submitting your life to some 'greater good' is really a supreme form of self-interest. Which it is, in a sense, because it offers one way (perhaps the only way) of reconciling yourself with death: the knowledge that something more important than your life will survive. From this perspective, what needs to be fought is the monstrously powerful instinct to believe that there is really nothing worse than death, and conversely nothing more important than survival, and therefore – because survival is, in the end, impossible – no real way of accepting life.

The philosopher Leszek Kołakowski expressed this very forcefully at the end of his essay 'The Revenge of the Sacred on Secular Culture':

Religion is man's way of accepting life as an inevitable defeat. That it is not an inevitable defeat is a claim that cannot be defended in good faith. One can, of course, disperse one's life over the contingencies of every day, but even then it is only a ceaseless and desperate desire to live, and finally a regret that one has not lived. One can accept life, and accept it, at the same time, as a defeat only if one accepts that there is a sense beyond that which is inherent in human history – if, in other words, one accepts the order of the sacred. A hypothetical world from which the sacred had been swept away would admit of only two possibilities: vain fantasy that recognises itself as such, or immediate satisfaction which exhausts itself. It would leave only the choice proposed by Baudelaire, between lovers of prostitutes and lovers of clouds: those who know only the satisfactions of the moment and are therefore contemptible, and those who lose themselves in otiose imaginings, and are therefore contemptible. Everything is then contemptible, and there is nothing more to be said. The conscience liberated from the sacred knows this, even if it conceals it from itself.

The principle Kołakowski employs here is simple enough: if 'accepting' or 'redeeming' your existence means anything, it's only if there's something beyond your existence to measure it against. Yet in spite of what he says about religion, the same argument could be put in less devout terms. 'Sacred' might stand for any sort of transcendent category – Love, Justice, Beauty, Truth, Goodness – whatever there is cutting across the contingent facts of our bodies and circumstantial ways of life; the 'extra-something' on top of material reality. The problem of how we justify art re-emerges here. The idea that art is the closest thing secular consciousness has to religious expression isn't uncommon, and it flatters artists. But obviously religion is never purely aesthetic, because it involves a truth-claim about the reality of the supernatural. In Pascal's thinking, art that isn't dedicated to God is merely another form of diversion, not serving truth but seeking to disguise it. However, if the truth is that there's nothing out there, no God and nothing sacred (however we understand the term), then it seems as though all that art *could* be is a diversion; a lie – and hence contemptible. A different way of putting the same point is that if an activity so clearly impractical as writing had any true justification, it would need to be something above practical concern, whether this was a supernatural God or an abstract ideal or something else. Since these things are immaterial, we can never be sure of them in the way we can be sure of physical reality, and so talking about them can easily seem empty or deluded. But for all that it isn't trivial. Although not everybody reads literature or even cares that fiction exists, the endless difficulty writers have justifying their work is more important than it might look, because it's essentially a route towards much deeper questions about the reality of ideals. There are good reasons for being shy about asking these sorts of questions. Still, the dilemma Kołakowski describes does not go away, and Houellebecq illustrates its horns well: if there is no greater good to serve (whatever it may be), the options seem to be either the unsustainable treadmill of hedonism, or a life wrapped up inside craven fantasies. In which case the general contempt Houellebecq sprays at existence is really just an orderly consequence of his materialism.

Rehearse all of the bile depressive realism aims at literature: aesthetic pleasure is pathetically fragile, wrecked by pain, hunger, lack of sleep, sexual frustration, or any other variety of basic bodily want, none of which it is capable of alleviating. Fiction does not fill bellies or raise roofs. Producing it barely pays bills. To write a novel, even quite a good novel, must seem absurdly trivial set against the manifest violence, injustice and suffering of the world. And even if creating literature could be defined as a social good of sorts (which maybe it can't), still it is hard to see how the bulk of time spent writing or reading couldn't be better invested in medicine or public organisation or something else practical, if social good is what is desired. How could anyone deny any of this? In particular, how could anyone deny that worrying about books is shamelessly decadent compared to, for example, appalling Third World hunger and poverty? So that to persist with writing in the face of the facts looks like a ridiculous article of faith ('I know perfectly well that writing is useless and self-indulgent, and yet nonetheless...'). You might construct an argument, following Žižek, to say the value of literature is illusory set against all the world's ills – but an illusion with power, a 'good lie'. That is still to call it a lie.

But it ought to be remembered that the injunction to forget about ideas and focus on 'real' problems invariably has something false about it, too. It is a way of hiding from the pain of not knowing what to think. For most of us, most of the time, that pain is not sharp – but when it is it is horrible and hard, and not abstract in the slightest. 'In every calm and reasonable person there is a hidden second person scared witless about death,' wrote Philip Roth. Ordinarily, it's only every so often we encounter this second inner person and 'the state of madness' they live in. But we can't avoid them completely. There are terrible things that happen in the world, and alongside them is the terror of our own death, and (equally inevitable) the deaths of everybody we care about. What could possibly be the 'right' thing to believe, in the face of such dreadful facts? Perhaps some form of faith is indispensable, but its indispensability might not be a refutation of depressive realism so much as an awesomely bleak punch-line to the whole business. Because in a sense pessimism remains perfectly correct: there is no way to protect yourself from the world, finally; and the ultimate indifference of the universe makes whatever beliefs we have about it seem completely irrelevant. Yet we can't help but believe. Henry Miller said life needs to be given meaning, because it so obviously has none. And this is just it: the core joke or paradox or calamity, or however you choose to see it, is that we go on – *need* to go on – projecting meaning onto what might very well be meaningless. This, too, is a writer's anxiety generalised: the worry that our stories are 'nothing but' stories, and that when we talk about ethics or ideals we are not saying anything true but things that only *sound* true; charming, empty fictions.

Kant admitted one of the difficulties in his moral philosophy was that, although it's possible to deduce using abstract reason that there is genuinely such a thing as moral duty, from the individual's limited perspective it's never possible to be certain that you are acting for the sake of your duty, even when you act in accordance with it. In other words, it is impossible to tell whether your intentions are pure, or whether you're really acting for the sake of some concealed, base desire, e.g. to flatter your vanity, or to impress your peers, or because being moral happens to serve your own selfish interests. If we're inclined to examine our behaviour honestly, it must very often seem this way – that our motivations are typically rather weak and petty, and our ends generally nothing better than pleasure and comfort. But Žižek puts an interesting spin on Kant's dilemma. He claims the tendency to read a selfish motivation into every idealistic act is itself a defence mechanism, a ruse to cover up the truly distressing idea that we might after all be acting 'for nothing': for the sake of high-flown values we are not even sure exist. In which case, the only genuinely ethical stance is to try and identify the worthiest things to belief in, and embrace them in their uncertainty. Similarly, Wallace suggested in one of his essays that literature ought to always exhibit a concern with 'what it is to be a human being – that is, how to be an actual *person*, someone whose life is informed by values and principles, instead of just an especially shrewd kind of self-preserving animal'. It is not a platitude. The point is that the very things which define human life – our values and principles – are also things we are left agonisingly uncertain about. The consequence is that to be an actual person is to be a very strange kind of creature, something undecided by nature.

'The truth is scandalous, but without it nothing has any value', wrote Houellebecq in a manifesto on the vocation of poetry ('To Stay Alive – A Method'). In the service of his art, he said, the poet must delve 'into the subjects that no one wants to hear about. ... Insist upon sickness, agony, ugliness. Speak of death, and of oblivion. Of jealousy, of indifference, of frustration, of the absence of love. Be abject, and you will be true.' Beneath these words is a deeply moral thought: the vital thing is not to be against happiness, but against *unthinking* happiness; optimism that edits out the parts of living no one wants to hear about. That is the task – to stay awake to the world, without despair. It may be impossible, but (thankfully) there is no way of knowing. 'You cannot love the truth and the world', claims Houellebecq in the same essay. Yet his advice to poets is also a subtle rebuke to depressive realism, whether he intended it or not. 'A dead poet does not write. Hence the importance of remaining alive.' Why stay alive for the sake of poetry? The answer Houellebecq gives is striking – not because he suddenly finds a way to make life seem acceptable, but because he affirms the idea that honesty can take us to places far stranger than pessimism. The writer's calling may seem 'painfully pointless' sometimes:

> To this, only one reply: ultimately, you know nothing about it. … You will never really know this part of yourself which compels you to write. You will know it only through contradictory forms which merely approach it. Egotism or devotion? Cruelty or compassion? Any of these possibilities could be argued for. Proof that, ultimately, you know nothing about it; thus, do not behave as if you did. Before your own ignorance, before this mysterious part of yourself, remain honest and humble.

That life is not an inevitable defeat is not a claim that can be defended in good faith. Not everyone is happy, or healthy, or loved – but everyone is caged in their own body, and in the deepest sense helpless over what happens to them, and everybody dies. In a certain state of mind that feels very like lucidity, the bad things appear so much more pertinent and insoluble and unutterably *real* that the idea of being sanguine or reasonable or 'intelligent' about them is almost hideous. But what's real is never really so clear. It is incredibly hard to bear this in mind. The great difficulty thinking about pessimism is that you reach a point where you become aware of how thoroughly empty or pretentious any appeals to moral abstractions can sound, but also (as Kołakowski says) that there is a sense in which we unmistakably *need* something 'sacred' to be true if we're not to feel contemptible. How you reconcile this demand with the equally important need to believe you aren't deluded is, finally, a matter for individual judgment, but at the very least it helps to be reminded (through art, or other means) that faith, worship and unjustified belief are always and already part of our lives. The most reliable defence against pessimism is the knowledge that pessimism, too, is unsure. 'Before your own ignorance, before this mysterious part of yourself, remain honest and humble.' In the end there is no theory, and this is also a sort of gift.

# Notes

1 Although as often as not (and there are one or two big exceptions) interviews report that Houellebecq is charming in person, something that seems incongruous at first but makes a sort of sense when you think about it – it's like the inverse of the cliché comedian who's completely wretched and horrible whenever he isn't on stage.

2 Interestingly, that judgment was part of Wallace's 1997 review of John Updike's *Toward the End of Time* in the *New York Observer*; the same John Updike who disapprovingly quoted Houellebecq's bit about all energy being sexual energy in the slightly pious notice he gave of *The Possibility of an Island* in the *New Yorker* in 2006.

3 In 2001, French courts agreed to hear a formal case brought against Houellebecq by four French Muslim organisations on the charge of racism, after he was quoted (inaccurately, he claims) in an interview promoting *Platform* saying that Islam was 'the most stupid of all religions'. The case was eventually dismissed, but in between the publication of *Platform* and his appearance in court two planes smashed into the World Trade Center, which obviously made Houellebecq's eye for subject-matter seem like an uncannily sharp one, whatever else.

4 For one minor example: hip-hop, a decidedly modern music. Hip-hop never seems right reproduced in a novel. Part of this, I think, is that a novel that reproduces a rap verse invariably writes the words out line-by-line, which is fine but palpably not how the music (which is, on the face of it, one of the most 'articulate' or 'wordy' types there is) makes itself felt – often the rhythm of a rap song pulls you along in spite of the fact that you usually can't really separate or understand many of the words if you aren't

already familiar with the verse. This pull isn't there on the page, although it is there on the radio, television, street corner, coming out of car-windows, i.e. all the everyday circumstances where one has the opportunity to hear rap music and compare it unfavourably to how it comes across inside a novel. Further minor example: Speaking personally, I find email exchanges written out in a novel almost unfailingly clunky and awkward, e.g. pp 497–502 of Franzen's *The Corrections* (2001). Is it that email, too, simply feels wrong and not-at-home on the printed page?

5 A personal example: when I'm out listening to music on my headphones, it's often hard to avoid the sensation that I'm the middle of a sound-tracked video.

6 'It seems to me that the intellectualization and aestheticizing of principles and values in this country is one of the things that's gutted our generation. All the things that my parents said to me, like "It's really important not to lie." OK, check, got it. I nod at that but I really don't feel it. Until I get to be about 30 and I realize that if I lie to you, I also can't trust you. I feel that I'm in pain, I'm nervous, I'm lonely and I can't figure out why. Then I realize, "Oh, perhaps the way to deal with this is really not to lie." The idea that something so simple and, really, so aesthetically uninteresting – which for me meant you pass over it for the interesting, complex stuff – can actually be nourishing in a way that arch, meta, ironic, PoMo stuff can't, that seems to me to be important.' –David Foster Wallace, interview with *Salon*, March 8th, 1996.

7 As mentioned, 'E Unibus Pluram' was written in 1990. It's still extremely relevant, which attests to how immobile the problems it talks about are, but there are a couple of then-and-now changes worth noting. One of these is to do with advertising trends, and perhaps helps to illuminate Fisher's idea of 'precorporation'. In 1990, the sort of advert that concerned Wallace was exemplified

by Burger King's 'Sometimes You Gotta Break the Rules' pitch for onion rings, i.e. a kind of ultra-commodified 'rebellion' that seems to totally defeat (while ironically mocking) any possibility of actually undermining the system. Compare that to Mastercard's ingenious 'For Everything Else There's Mastercard' campaign of more recent years, where the price of products (plane ticket/video camera/child's bicycle) is directly juxtaposed with the more profound, 'priceless' joys they facilitate (flying home in time to record your son's very first bicycle ride/experiencing the true meaning of Christmas). The conceit was brilliant: the adverts were catchy, witty, charmingly self-deprecating, and, on the face of it, also expounding some pretty admirable values about the relative worth of money and material trappings to things like community and human warmth. So what is there to dislike? Well, there's still the standard commercial desire to try and induce a kind of anxiously compelling self-consciousness in the target audience (*viz*, am I spending the money the right way? Do my purchases facilitate the important things in life as best they might? How much of my life corresponds to the admirable human ideals depicted by the concerned people at Mastercard?), which adds a faint but still unpleasantly competitive edge to the whole enterprise of finding personal meaning and fulfilment, plus it's still fantastic and unrealistic in the way of all advertising – but basically the issue is that, however nice and agreeable the advert is, fundamentally it does not have your best interests at heart. Its reason for being is to get you to give Mastercard money, and whether or not this helps you to experience happiness and self-worth is an irrelevance. The fact that such worthy goals are used in a sales pitch is – even just on a very slight, subconscious level – hurtful and depressing.

Point being, just as the laudable desire to rebel against what's fake can be twisted around to sell onion rings, the (good, true) belief that you shouldn't spend too much time worrying about comparatively unimportant things like adverts can be hijacked to sell credit cards. In a way, the difficulty is how much we agree with the values on show. (A similar thing is true of 'green' capitalism.) The feeling it inspires, speaking personally, is almost paradoxical, something like being caught between the need to recognise that certain values are good even if advertising says they're good, and the need to recognise that what's importantly worthwhile and truly valuable just in some fundamental sense *cannot be* what advertising says it is.

8 Possibly this is the reason artists and intellectuals, people who spend a higher proportion of time everyday inside their heads, are more than averagely prone to hypochondria – a disease of the imagination, after all.

9 For a sign of how tired Houellebecq's bile is at this point, consider Daniel25's observation that the chief of the human tribe is wearing an 'Ibiza Beach' T-shirt while he presides over a grotesque, blood-soaked carnival – not only thumping the reader over the head with an unbelievably crude metaphor, but asking us to believe that this Ibiza T-shirt was able to survive the *two thousand years* between the apocalypse and Daniel25's journey in order to arrive at such a richly symbolic position.

10 In fairness to Wallace, he never intended for the Kenyon address to be published – it only appeared in print after his death in 2008 – and it's necessarily a very simplified expression of his thinking. Zadie Smith's comment about the speech (in *Changing My Mind*, 2009) is worth bearing in mind. She said that it's 'hard to think of a less appropriate portrait of [Wallace] than as a dispenser of convenient pearls of wisdom, placed in your palm, so that you needn't go through any struggle yourself. ...the real worth of that speech... is as a diving board into his fiction, his fiction being his truest response to the difficulty of staying conscious and alive, day in and day out.'

Contemporary culture has eliminated both the concept of the public and the figure of the intellectual. Former public spaces – both physical and cultural – are now either derelict or colonized by advertising. A cretinous anti-intellectualism presides, cheerled by expensively educated hacks in the pay of multinational corporations who reassure their bored readers that there is no need to rouse themselves from their interpassive stupor. The informal censorship internalized and propagated by the cultural workers of late capitalism generates a banal conformity that the propaganda chiefs of Stalinism could only ever have dreamt of imposing. Zer0 Books knows that another kind of discourse – intellectual without being academic, popular without being populist – is not only possible: it is already flourishing, in the regions beyond the striplit malls of so-called mass media and the neurotically bureaucratic halls of the academy. Zer0 is committed to the idea of publishing as a making public of the intellectual. It is convinced that in the unthinking, blandly consensual culture in which we live, critical and engaged theoretical reflection is more important than ever before.